Rails-to-Trails

Connecticut, Rhode Island, Massachusetts, Vermont, New Hampshire, Maine

"Recreation trails are one of America's great outdoor secrets, but probably won't be for much longer thanks to the Rails-to-Trails Conservancy guidebook series. Now adventurers of all abilities have an excellent guide to help them enjoy all that the paths have to offer."

—Stephen Madden, Editor-in-Chief, *Outdoor Explorer*

"There's no better guide for these multipurpose trails. Like the Rails-to-Trails system, this series is a service that's long overdue."

—Sarah Parsons, Associate Editor, *Sports Afield*

Help Us Keep This Guide Up to Date

Every effort has been made by the author and editors to make this guide as accurate and useful as possible. However, many things can change after a guide is published—hiking trails are rerouted, establishments close, phone numbers change, facilities come under new management, and so on.

We would love to hear from you concerning your experiences with this guide and how you feel it could be improved and kept up to date. While we may not be able to respond to all comments and suggestions, we'll take them to heart and we'll also make certain to share them with the author. Please send your comments and suggestions to the following address:

The Globe Pequot Press
Reader Response/Editorial Department
P.O. Box 480
Guilford, CT 06437

Or you may e-mail us at:

editorial@globe-pequot.com

Thanks for your input, and happy travels!

Great Rail-Trails Series

THE OFFICIAL

Rails-to-Trails

CONSERVANCY GUIDEBOOK

Connecticut ▼ Rhode Island ▼ Massachusetts
Vermont ▼ New Hampshire ▼ Maine

by
Cynthia Mascott

The
Globe
Pequot
Press

Guilford, Connecticut

Rails-to-Trails Conservancy is a registered trademark of Rails-to-Trails Conservancy.

Cover illustration: Neal Aspinall
Cover design: Nancy Freeborn
Text design: Lesley Weissman-Cook
Maps: Tim Kissel/Trailhead Graphics, Inc., copyright © The Globe Pequot Press
Photo credits: pages xxi, 1, 6, 16, 20, 23, 72, 78, 87, 92, 97, 123, 159, 178, 182, 185, 188, 192, 193 by Karen-Lee Ryan; all other photos by Cynthia Mascott

Library of Congress Cataloging-in-Publication Data
Mascott, Cynthia.
   The official Rails-to-Trails Conservancy guidebook. Connecticut, Rhode Island, Massachusetts, Vermont, New Hampshire, Maine / by Cynthia Mascott. — 1st ed.
     p. cm. — (Great rail-trails series)
   ISBN 0-7627-0449-7
   1. Rail-trails—New England—Guidebooks. 2. Outdoor recreation—New England—Guidebooks. 3. New England—Guidebooks. I. Rails-to-Trails Conservancy. II. Title. III. Series.

GV191.42.N3 M28 2000
917.404'44—dc21   00-039372

Manufactured in the United States of America
First Edition/Sixth Printing

CAUTION
The Globe Pequot Press assumes no liability for accidents happening to or injuries sustained by readers who engage in the activities described in this book.

This book is dedicated to Bruce Emerson and Margaret Maes for their steadfast friendship and wonderful sense of humor.

CONTENTS

MASSACHUSETTS

NEW HAMPSHIRE

RHODE ISLAND

ACKNOWLEDGMENTS

This book could not have been completed without the companionship of Bruce Emerson and Margaret Maes, who suffered through the process of finding the rail-trails and then shared my delight in exploring them. I would like to thank my sister, Holly Mascott Nadler, for our various misadventures on the Cape and for the stilling of our hearts at the Christmas Tree Shoppe. Terry Hansberry was a real trouper and helped me with all things New Hampshirian. I would also like to thank my cousin Deborah Mascott and her husband, Steven Malchman, for their trip along the Farmington Canal Trail. My parents, Trina and Laurence Mascott, could not have been more supportive even though they were on the other side of the continent. Finally, I would like to thank all of the park rangers, district managers, and rail-trail enthusiasts who helped me through the process of writing this book.

INTRODUCTION

O ur pace is so fast. In the ever-changing and evolving world of
technology, we literally cannot keep up with the times. Once
upon a time, the train seemed like the epitome of the modern world.
Sleek and bold trains were our nation's pride and joy and symbolized
the possibilities of a world beyond the one in which we lived. Connecting large cities and small towns, used for transportation and for
the shipping of goods, the train was the pulse of the nation.

But times change. With the advent of the car and the building of
mass highways, trains became a secondary form of transportation.
And dreams die. Railroad tracks were abandoned. Nature took over
and where once a track split through the woods, only a ghost of the
track remained.

Enter the Rails-to-Trails Conservancy, a group of outdoor enthusiasts who began the arduous task of transforming the railroad tracks
to nature trails. Banding together with other conservation groups, the
Rails-to-Trails Conservancy removed railroad tracks and molded the

Along the Burlington Waterfront Bikeway in Vermont.

trails into wonderful paths running through urban and rural areas.

There is something remarkable about traveling the nation in pursuit of the abandoned railroad track now converted to greenways, bicycle paths, and nature paths. What better way to see the country than by traversing these rail beds?

New England is where our nation began. It was in the Northeastern United States where the railroad was first introduced. The railroads that once crisscrossed New England are now being transformed into rail-trails. From the remote regions of Maine and New Hampshire, to the more populated cities of Providence and Boston, rail-trails are part of today's culture.

Where once a dream was lost, it now is recovered with the advent of more and more rail-trails. So, hop on your bike or horse, put on a pair of hiking boots, or lace those snowshoes. It's time to explore New England's rail-trails!

A Little New England Rail History

New England's rail history is as rich as it is varied. Railroads once crisscrossed our nation with a vast maze of tracks. Main lines con-

Old trains remain at the Raymond Station on the Rockingham Recreational Trail in New Hampshire.

nected the cities, and smaller lines reached the less populated communities. There were passenger lines and cargo lines. Locomotives brought in coal and cotton and manufactured goods were sent out to the rest of the country. The very pulse of the nation was measured by its railroad commerce.

The first New England railroad was constructed in 1805, in Boston's Beacon Hill. Between 1830 and 1860, the number of rail lines continued to grow, and much of the Northeast was connected with miles and miles of track. In some cases, greed and competition created unnecessary duplicate rail systems. By the 1870s, many of the independent railroads were consolidated into fourteen larger systems. According to Donald Dale Karr in his book *The Lost Railroads of New England,* the train depot replaced the village green as the center of New England towns in the latter part of the nineteenth century. At the pinnacle of the railroading era, nearly 300,000 miles of track spanned the nation, a network six times larger than today's interstate highway system.

The advent of the automobile in the early 1900s brought a rapid decline to the rail system. Railroad companies began to abandon some of the duplicate trackage in the 1920s. The Great Depression of the 1930s further escalated the decline of New England railroads. Many of the region's factories closed or moved south. Car ownership became more and more popular and many passenger service trains were shut down. There was a burst of newfound energy during World War II. The railroad companies converted their trains from steam to diesel and passenger and freight service rose. But the resurgence of interest in the railways was short lived. By the 1960s, the railroad system virtually collapsed as the country began building the freeways and highways that now connect our nation. Today, less than half of the original railroad network exists. It is estimated that more than 2,000 miles of track are abandoned every year.

The history of New England railroads parallels that of the rest of the country. It is a story of dreams and folly. Where once railroads dominated our landscape, their tracks now lie abandoned. The question remained, what to do with all those miles of railroad tracks?

Enter the Rails-to-Trails Conservancy, an environmental group that since 1986 has campaigned to convert the railroad tracks to nature paths.

The History of the Rails-to-Trails Conservancy

The beauty of the Rails-to-Trails Conservancy (RTC) is that by converting the railroad rights-of-way for public use, it has not only preserved a part of our nation's history, but it also allows a variety of outdoor enthusiasts to enjoy the paths and trails.

Bicyclists, in-line skaters, nature lovers, hikers, equestrians, and cross-country skiers can enjoy the trails as well as railroad history buffs. Many of the trails are wheelchair accessible. Throughout New England, there are fifty active RTC trails. Each year, additional trails are added. You can find trails near cities and rural trails far from the maddening crowd. In many ways, we have come full circle. By preserving part of our history, we can enjoy the trails as if time stood still.

The concept of preserving these valuable corridors and converting them into multiuse public trails began in the Midwest, where railroad abandonments were most widespread. Once the tracks came out, people started using the corridors for walking and hiking while exploring railroad relics ranging from train stations and mills to bridges and tunnels.

Although many people agreed with the great new concept, the reality of actually converting abandoned railroad corridors into public trails was a much greater challenge. From the late 1960s until the early 1980s, many rail-trail efforts failed as corridors were lost to development, sold to the highest bidder, or broken into pieces.

In 1983, Congress enacted an amendment to the National Trails System Act directing the Interstate Commerce Commission to allow about-to-be abandoned railroad lines to be "railbanked," or set aside for future transportation use while being used as trails in the interim. In essence, this law preempts rail corridor abandonment, keeping the corridors intact for trail use and any possible future use.

This powerful new piece of legislation made it easier for agencies and organization to acquire rail corridors for trails, but many projects still failed because of short deadlines, lack of information, and local opposition to trails.

In 1986, the Rails-to-Trails Conservancy formed to provide a national voice for the creation of rail-trails. RTC quickly developed a strategy to preserve the largest amount of rail corridor in the shortest period of time: a national advocacy program to defend the new railbanking law in the courts and in Congress, coupled with a direct project-assistance program to help public agencies and local rail-trail groups overcome the challenges of converting a rail into a trail.

The strategy is working. In 1986, the Rails-to-Trails Conservancy knew of only seventy-five rail-trails and ninety projects in the works. Today, there are more than a thousand rail-trails and many additional projects are under way. The RTC vision of creating an interconnected network of trails across the country is becoming a reality.

The thriving rails-to-trails movement has created more than

Watch for wildlife along the Beebe Spur Rail-Trail in Vermont.

7,700 miles of public trails for a wide range of users. People across the country are now realizing the incredible benefits of the rail-trails.

Benefits of Rail-Trails

Rail-trails are flat or have gentle grades, making them perfect for multiple users ranging from walkers and bicyclists to in-line skaters and people with disabilities. In snowy climates, people enjoy cross-country skiing, snowmobiling, and other snow activities on the trails.

In urban areas, rail-trails act as linear greenways through developed areas, efficiently providing much-needed recreation space while serving as utilitarian transportation corridors. They link neighborhoods and workplaces and connect congested areas to open spaces. In many cities and suburbs, rail-trails are used for commuting to work, school, and shopping.

In rural areas, rail-trails can provide a significant stimulus to local businesses. People who use trails often spend money on food, beverages, camping, hotels, bed-and-breakfasts, bicycle rentals, souvenirs, and other items. Studies have shown that trail users have generated as much as $1.25 million annually for a town through which a trail passes.

Rail-trails preserve historic structures, such as train stations, bridges, tunnels, mills, factories, and canals. These structures shelter an important piece of history and enhance the trail experience.

Wildlife enthusiasts can enjoy the rail-trails, which are home to birds, plants, wetlands, and small and large mammals. Many rail-trails serve as plant and animal conservation corridors, and, in some cases, endangered species can be found in habitats located along the route.

Recreation, transportation, historic preservation, economic revitalization, open space conservation, and wildlife preservation—these are just some of the many benefits of rail-trails and the reasons why people love them.

The strongest argument for the rail-to-trails movement, however, is ultimately about the human spirit. It's about the dedication of individuals who have a dream and follow that vision so that other people can enjoy the fruits of their labor.

How to Get Involved

If you really enjoy rail-trails, there are opportunities to join the movement to save abandoned rail corridors and to create more trails. Donating even a small amount of your time can help get more trails up and going. Here are some ways you can help the effort:

- Write a letter to your city, county, or state elected official in favor of pro-trail legislation. You can also write a letter to the editor of your local newspaper highlighting a trail or trail project.
- Attend a public hearing to voice support for a local trail.
- Volunteer to plant flowers or trees along an existing trail or spend several hours helping a cleanup crew on a nearby rail-trail project.
- Lead a hike along an abandoned corridor with your friends or a community group.
- Become an active member on a trail effort in your area. Many groups host trail events, undertake fund-raising campaigns, publish brochures and newsletters, and carry out other activities to promote a trail or project. Virtually all of these efforts are completed by volunteers and they are always looking for another helping hand.

THE EAST COAST GREENWAY

(Reprinted with permission of the East Coast Greenway)

The East Coast Greenway will be the nation's first long-distance, city-to-city, multimodal transportation corridor for cyclists, joggers, hikers, the sight impaired, and other nonmotorized users. Our goal is to connect existing and planned trails that are locally owned and managed to form a continuous, safe, green route—easily identified by the public through signage, maps, user's guides, and common services. The route will be at least 80 percent off-road, using waterfront esplanades, park paths, abandoned railroads, canal towpaths, and parkway corridors. It will serve cyclists, joggers, hikers, skaters, equestrians, the sight impaired, people in wheelchairs, and other nonmotorized users. We are presently working hard to develop the entire trail from Canada to Key West, Florida. Our route will be an urban alternative to the Appalachian Trail, located in the shadows of skyscrapers and within suburban greenspace, but also in surprisingly rural areas that still exist between our East Coast cities. It will enable residents to travel short distances from their homes to local points of interest, and tourists to travel for a few days or even weeks to visit the rich store of history and culture within the East Coast region. Perhaps people will set a goal to travel the entire length of the greenway over a period of years. While seeking the most direct feasible route between cities, we also value a route offering an interesting, varied experience. It will link with a host of other greenways and trails being developed within the region, forming a true greenway network functioning much like the interstate highway system.

Whatever your time allows, get involved. The success of a community's rail-trail depends upon the level of citizen participation. The Rails-to-Trails Conservancy enjoys both local and national support. By joining the RTC you will get discounts on all of its publications and merchandise while supporting the largest national trails organization in the United States. To become a member, use the order form at the back of the book.

How to Use Rail-Trails

By design, rail-trails accommodate a variety of trail users. While this is generally one of the many benefits of rail-trails, it also can lead to occasional conflicts among trail users. Everyone should take responsibility to ensure trail safety by following a few simple trail etiquette guidelines.

One of the most basic etiquette rules is, "Wheels yield to heels." The figure below indicates the correct protocol for yielding right-of-way. Bicyclists (and in-line skaters) yield to other users; pedestrians yield to equestrians.

Generally, this means that you need to warn users (to whom you are yielding) of your presence. If, as a bicyclist, you fail to warn a walker that you are about to pass, the walker could step in front of you, causing an accident that could have been prevented. Similarly, it is best to slow down and warn an equestrian of your presence. A horse can be startled by a bicycle, so make verbal contact with the rider and be sure it is safe to pass.

Here are some other guidelines you should follow to promote trail safety:

- Obey all trail rules posted at trailheads.
- Stay to the right except when passing.
- Pass slower traffic on their left; yield to oncoming traffic when passing.
- Give a clear warning signal when passing.
- Always look ahead and behind when passing.
- Travel at a responsible speed.
- Keep pets on a leash.
- Do not trespass on private property.
- Move off the trail surface when stopped to allow others to pass.
- Yield to other trail users when entering and crossing the trail.

- Do not disturb the wildlife.
- Do not swim in areas not designated for swimming.
- Watch out for traffic when crossing the street.
- Obey all traffic signals.

How to Use This Book

At the beginning of each state, you will find a map showing the location of the state's rail-trails. The text description of every trail begins with the following information:

- **Name**: The official name of the rail-trail.
- **Activities:** A list of icons tell you what kinds of activities are appropriate for each trail.
- **Location:** The county or counties through which the trail passes.
- **Length:** The length of the trail, including how many miles are currently open, and for those trails that are built on partially abandoned corridors, the number of miles actually on the rail line.
- **Surface:** The materials that make up the rail-trail vary from trail to trail. This heading describes each trail's surface. Materials range from asphalt and crushed stone to the significantly more rugged original railroad ballast.
- **Wheelchair access:** Some of the rail-trails are wheelchair accessible. This allows physically challenged individuals the opportu-

One of the many pleasant water views along the Falmouth Shining Sea Path in Massachusetts.

nity to explore the rail-trails with family and friends.

- **Difficulty:** The rail-trails range from easy to difficult, depending on the grade of the trail and the general condition of the trail.
- **Food:** The book will indicate the names of the towns near the rail-trails in which restaurants and fast food shops are available.
- **Rest rooms:** If a rest room is available near the trail, the book will provide you with its location.
- **Seasons:** Most of the trails are open year-round; however, some close during the winter months.
- **Access and parking:** The book will provide you with directions to the rail-trails and parking availability.
- **Rentals:** Some of the rail-trails have bicycle shops and skating stores nearby. This will help you with bike or skate rental information or, if you are having problems with your equipment, you can have it checked out at the store.
- **Transportation:** Occasionally public transportation is available to a town through which the trail passes.
- **Contact:** The name and contact information for each trail manager is listed here. The selected contacts are generally responsible for managing the trail and can provide additional information about the trail and its condition.
- **Map:** The main rail-trails featured in this book include basic maps for your convenience. It's recommended, however, that street maps, topographic maps such as USGS quads, or a state atlas be used to supplement the maps in this book.
- **Mile-by-mile description:** The major rail-trails featured will have a mile-by-mile description allowing you the chance to anticipate the experience of the trail. So let's get going!

Key to Activities Icons

 Backpacking

 Mountain Biking

 Bird-watching

 Paddlesports

 Camping

 Road Bicycling

 Cross-country Skiing

 Running

 Fishing

 Swimming

 Historic Sites

 Walking/Dayhiking

 Horseback Riding

 Wildlife Viewing

 In-line Skating

Key to Map Icons

P Parking

R Rentals

I Information

A Camping

Rest Rooms

Rails-to-Trails

CONNECTICUT

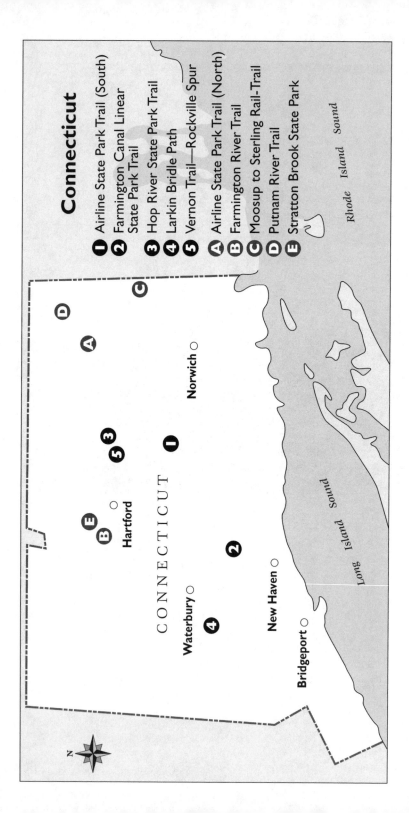

Connecticut

1 Airline State Park Trail (South)
2 Farmington Canal Linear State Park Trail
3 Hop River State Park Trail
4 Larkin Bridle Path
5 Vernon Trail—Rockville Spur
A Airline State Park Trail (North)
B Farmington River Trail
C Moosup to Sterling Rail-Trail
D Putnam River Trail
E Stratton Brook State Park

INTRODUCTION

While small in size (only Rhode Island and Delaware are smaller), Connecticut is large in beauty. From the Connecticut coastline to its interior forests and hills, the state bespeaks grace. The Nutmeg State has more than eighty lakes and ponds and 300 miles of rivers and streams.

Connecticut's first European settlers arrived almost 400 years ago. The Dutch settlement of Kievit's Hoeck (now Old Saybrook) was founded in 1623. The following year, the English trading post of Wethersfield was incorporated. In 1635, Reverend Thomas Hooker and his followers settled in Hartford to flee oppressive Puritan laws in Massachusetts.

More than 30,000 men enlisted in the Continental Army to fight for their freedom during the American Revolution. And the Yankee spirit prevails in the state today!

Take time to explore the coast. Mystic is particularly charming, with its seaside ambience and the maritime history of Mystic Seaport, which depicts life in a nineteenth-century New England whaling community. Westward along the coast, in New Haven, is prestigious Yale University. The oldest of the college's ivy-covered buildings, Connecticut Hall, was built in 1752 and housed Nathan Hale during his studies in the late 1700s.

Hartford, Connecticut's capital and largest city, has long been associated with the insurance business. While the town is modern, its historical roots are evidenced by downtown's Ancient Burying Grounds. The oldest gravestone dates to 1663. Also of interest are the Hartford homes of Mark Twain and of Harriet Beecher Stowe, author of *Uncle Tom's Cabin*.

The southwestern corner of the state is one of the most affluent neighborhoods in the United States. Mansions abound here, many of them home to the rich and famous who commute to New York City or are employed at the Fortune 500 industries that have set up their offices in Fairfield County.

In contrast, the northeastern corner of the state is rural. It is a particularly pretty area to visit in the spring, when the dogwood and fruit trees are in bloom and the rolling hills are blanketed with green grass.

Connecticut's rail-trails offer plenty of adventure and fun. Enjoy the views of the Lyman's Viaduct, which spans some 1,100 feet and is more than 150 feet high and 50 feet wide. The Farmington Greenway follows an old canal that once provided transportation for large barges as they passed through the waters. The Hop River State Park and the nearby Vernon Trail are just a short hop from downtown Hartford. Other rail-trails of special interest include the Moosup to Sterling Rail-Trail, the Middlebury Greenway, Stratton State Park, and the Farmington River Trail.

With thirteen opened rail-trails and an additional twenty-seven trails projected in the state, Connecticut holds the promise of more than 200 miles of rail-trails.

TOP RAIL-TRAILS

1 Airline State Park Trail (South)

Panoramic views of the surrounding Connecticut hills and valleys characterize the Airline State Park Trail. Its most dramatic features are its two hidden viaducts, which offer expansive views of the scenery below.

Activities:

Location: New London and Middlesex Counties

Length: 5 miles

Surface: Original ballast and gravel

Wheelchair access: No special wheelchair facilities

Difficulty: Moderate

Food: Limited eateries and convenience stores are available along State Route 16.

Rest rooms: Rest rooms are available at various convenience stores and gas stations along State Route 16.

Seasons: Open year-round.

Access and parking: From State Route 2 (southeast of Hartford), take exit 16 and head south on State Route 149 about 5 miles to State Route 16 (Middletown Road). Turn right. Travel west on Route 16 for about 2 miles and turn right onto Comstock Bridge Road. Pass a covered bridge, turn right, and follow the road up the hill. At 1.2 miles is a set of yellow gates where a parking area can accommodate about a dozen cars.

Rentals:
- Rainbow Cycle, 385 Valley Street, Willimantic, CT; (860) 423–7182.
- Scott's Cyclery, 1171 Main Street, Willimantic, CT; (860) 423–8889.

Contact: William Mattioli, Water Safety Coordinator, State Parks Division, State of Connecticut Department of Environmental Protection, Hartford, CT 06106-5127; (860) 424–3209; fax (860) 424–4070; http://dep.state.ct.us/.

· · · · · · · · · · · · · · · · · · · ·

The Airline State Park Trail has several nice features. It takes the traveler past rolling hills and valleys before opening up to expansive views atop the trail's two viaducts left over from railroading days.

The Airline State Park Trail receives its name from the railroad that sped passengers between New York and Boston. The New York and Boston Railroad Company began developing the railroad line, but it was eventually completed by the Boston and New York Airline Railroad. Dozens of bridges and viaducts were constructed to span the rivers and valleys in central Connecticut. Two enormous viaducts, each more than 1,000 feet long, were built near East Hampton in the early 1870s. Eventually, the viaducts could not support the weight of heavier trains and early in the twentieth century they were completely filled in with rock. While much of the land is now in public ownership (the northern section was acquired in the 1960s and the southern section was acquired in the 1970s), dozens of impassable bridges have stalled trail development for many years. However, 5 miles of trail are currently open to the public.

To get to the trail from the parking lot, head to the left, navigating around some large boulders and a gate. The trail is densely wooded initially, but within 0.2 mile, it begins to open up as it approaches the Lyman Viaduct. You know you are crossing the viaduct when huge chunks of ballast cover the trail's surface. This surface is more conducive to hiking and horseback riding than to mountain biking.

Equestrians make up one of the largest user groups of the Airline Trail.

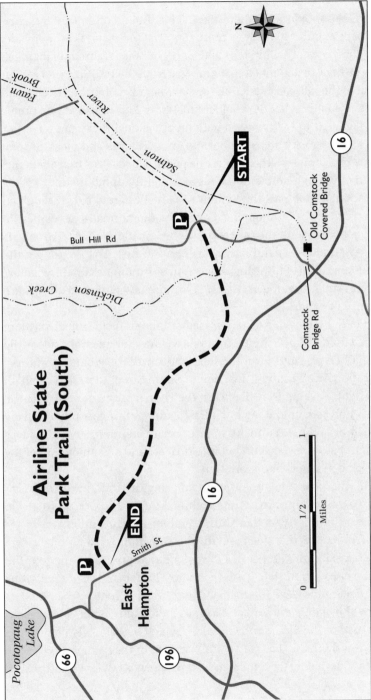

Bicyclists should walk their bikes. This mound of ballast and gravel spans about 1,100 feet, is more than 150 high, and is 50 feet wide.

The views of rolling hills and valleys to the left are breathtaking. The strip of rusted metal that emerges from the trail surface is an artifact of the railroad years. Take some time traversing the viaduct and try to visualize what the viaduct must have looked like at one time.

The next mile is wooded with an occasional rocky cut on either side. These rocky areas are havens for wild ferns and moss. Several horse trails traverse the trail at this point. The trail's surface remains relatively rough here and travels at a slightly uphill incline.

About a mile past the Lyman's Viaduct the trail cuts through an extensive rocky outcropping, blasted by the railroad's developers to gain passage. Soon the trail reaches the Rapallo Viaduct. This one is longer (1,400 feet) and narrower than the first. You do not get the same sensation of towering above your surroundings on this viaduct, but it is still intriguing to cross. The surface is again made up of sharp chunks of ballast.

On the opposite side of the viaduct, the trail continues for more than a mile to Smith Street. It passes wetlands on the right side while a small creek gurgles on the left. The surface is generally chunky and sporadically sandy. Just before Smith Street there is a pond on the right. Parking is available on the shores of the pond. While the trail continues into downtown East Hampton, it gets progressively narrower and more difficult to proceed. In addition, several bridges are not passable. The best bet is to turn around and enjoy the rolling hills and viaducts one more time.

If you have time, it is worth exploring the trail on the opposite side of the parking area. After backtracking to the parking area, you can continue west on the Airline Trail for nearly 2 miles.

The trail on this side is relatively wide and raised up on a ridge. After passing the first series of rocky outcroppings on the left, the trail passes a waterfall. The wooded trail offers a mix of coniferous and deciduous trees interspersed with walls of rock.

Within a mile the surface becomes quite sandy. Soon you can hear the rush of the Salmon River below, which occasionally comes into view on the right. The trail skirts the edge of the Salmon River State Forest. Just before the 2-mile mark, the trail ends at a fenced-off bridge.

The Farmington Canal Trail is a popular destination for people of all ages. The trail has a wide paved surface, mileage and kilometer markers, benches, solid wood bridges, and signs at road crossings indicating upcoming towns.

Activities:

Location: New Haven County

Length: 6 miles; an additional 2 miles of trail are scheduled to be added in October 2000.

Surface: Asphalt

Wheelchair access: Yes

Difficulty: Easy

Food: Restaurants can be found along Route 10 in Cheshire.

Rest rooms: There are rest rooms at the end of the trail at Sleeping Giant State Park.

Seasons: Open year-round.

Access and parking: From Hartford, take I–84 south to the intersection of I–691. Take I–691 east for 3 miles until you reach the exit for Route 10, Milldale. Take a right onto Route 10 and head south 5 miles into Cheshire. Proceed a short distance to Cornwall Street. Turn right onto Cornwall. The trailhead is at the intersection of Willow and Cornwall Streets. A small parking lot is located here.

Rentals:
- Alpine Ski Works, 1064 South Main Street, Cheshire, CT; (860) 272–6614.
- The Bike Rack, 1650 Whitney Avenue, Hamden, CT; (860) 281–6660.

Contact: Farmington River Trail, Daniel Dickinson, Park and Forest Supervisor, State of Connecticut Department of Environmental Protection, 178 South Swamp Road, Farmington, CT 06032; (203) 677–1819.

· ·

The Farmington Canal Linear State Park Trail offers visitors both enjoyable countryside and the historic Farmington Canal. The fully restored Lock 12 Historical Park is of special interest to history buffs.

Jogging is an option along the Farmington Canal Trail.

The Farmington Canal opened in 1828 after five years of construction. It connected New Haven, Connecticut, with Northampton, Massachusetts. Within two decades, however, railroads had surpassed and replaced canal transportation, and the New Haven Railroad was constructed along the former canal towpath. The railroad line operated continuously under a series of owners until it was damaged by a flood in 1982. The state then acquired the line and began work on the Farmington Canal Linear State Park Trail.

As the trail begins, the old canal is located on the left side of the trail corridor. It's hard to imagine that this narrow band of water was once a powerful force in America's early transportation network. Now just a few feet across, the canal during its years of operation spanned more than 30 feet, enabling large barges to pass. Ducks, geese, and turtles are the canal's primary users today.

At the 1-mile mark, the trail passes Higgins Road at grade. A half-mile farther along, the path crosses Brooksvale Road, leading to a parking lot signaling Lock 12 Historical Park. Recently restored to

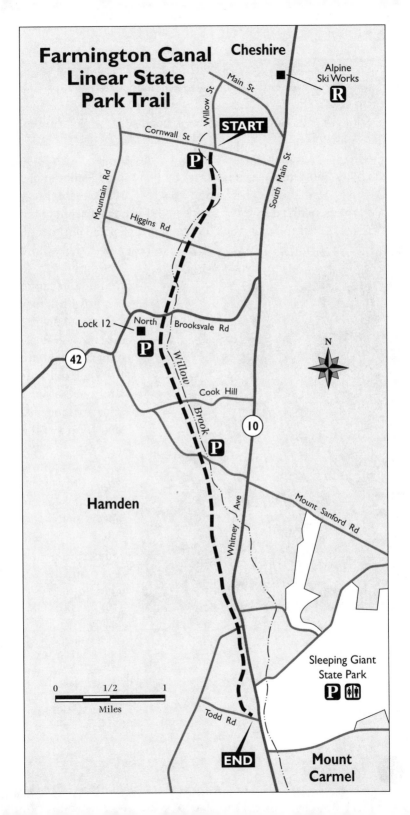

its original appearance, Canal Lock 12 is a popular stopping point. A small path leads directly to the lock, which once helped raise and lower boats on the canal. A small locktender's house still stands here. Soon after the lock, Willow Brook begins to parallel the trail on the right side.

During the summer of 1995, the trail was extended beyond the 3-mile mark and a new parking lot was built at Mount Sanford Road (3.3 miles). Despite the construction, this section is more densely wooded than the first 3 miles. A tree farm is located adjacent to the trail's left side near mile marker 4. Route 10, which parallels the trail, now comes into view briefly.

The next mile is a mix of homes and woods, while the last mile closely parallels Route 10. The trail currently ends at Todd Street, a short distance north of the entrance to Sleeping Giant State Park. This park, which offers picnic tables, grills, rest rooms, and hiking, equestrian, and cross-country skiing trails, is an excellent place to stop and relax.

A Connecticut family enjoys fun on the trail.

3 Hop River State Park Trail

Located within a half-hour's drive of the city of Hartford, the Hop River Trail offers a rugged hiking or mountain-biking experience through central Connecticut woodlands, with several small towns and a state park along the way.

Activities:

Location: Hartford and Tolland Counties

Length: 19 miles

Surface: Gravel and original ballast, including cinder, coarse gravel, and rocks

Wheelchair access: None

Difficulty: Difficult

Food: There are plenty of restaurants and fast-food establishments in Vernon.

Rest rooms: Valley Falls Park

Seasons: Open year-round.

Access and parking: From Hartford, take I–84 east and take exit 64-65 (Routes 30 and 83). Turn right at the end of the ramp. Travel on Route 30 north toward Vernon Center for a short distance to Dobson Street. Turn right onto Dobson, cross over I–84, and proceed another 0.3 mile to Church Street. Turn left onto Church and park at the trailhead.

Rentals:

- The Bike Shop, 681 Main Street, Manchester, CT; (860) 647–1027.
- The Cycle Center, 30 Post Road Plaza, Vernon, CT; (860) 872–7740.

Contact: Hop River State Park Trail, Joe Hickey, Environmentalist, Department of Environmental Protection, 79 Elm Street, Hartford, CT 06106-1632; (860) 424–3202; fax (860) 424–4070.

. . . .

Like many other Connecticut rail-trails, the Hop River State Park Trail is in various states of development. Undecked and missing bridges pose the most obvious obstacles, but the trail is generally passable—and very scenic.

The Hartford, Providence, and Fishkill Railroad operated this line from Rhode Island to the Hudson River. The line carried passengers and freight, including milk from nearby farms. Some local residents even took the train to school and back when the nearest high school was in Willimantic. After a storm in August 1955, the line was closed for passenger service. By 1970, freight was also discontinued. The State Department of Transportation acquired the corridor in the early 1970s and it has been used as a trail ever since. A recent cooperative agreement with a local National Guard unit helped resurface the section of the trail from Tunnel Road to the Bolton town line. The state hopes to forge similar cooperative agreements in the future.

The trail begins at a steady climb as you head toward a crossing at Tunnel Road just past the 1-mile mark. Here, you can see cars slowly passing underneath you; although you will not be able to see it, you are on top of a one-lane tunnel that carries car traffic under the rail-trail. The National Guard installed a new hard-packed crushed-stone surface in 1995, which begins just after Tunnel Road and continues for about 2.5 miles. The trail continues on an incline and onto a ridge veering right toward Valley Falls Park.

At the 2-mile mark, a pond is visible on the left. Located in Valley Falls Park, the pond is open to swimming during the summer months. A rest room, swing set, and picnic table are available in the park, but they're about 70 feet below the trail. Follow the blue-blazed hiking trail, which leads left off the trail through the trees and downhill to the park.

Rocky outcroppings generally line the right side of the trail for more than a mile, leading toward Bolton Notch State Park. There are no services available in the 70-acre park. There are, however, rumors of a secret cave on the premises! Beyond 3.5 miles the trail passes a pavilion, which is located on private property. By now the surface has returned to its more rugged original ballast as it continues gradually uphill. The surface is likely to be wet in areas that don't get much sun.

In about a mile, the trail passes Bolton Notch Pond before reaching a massive concrete tunnel. The tunnel often has standing water inside, and is likely to turn into a stream after a storm. Plan on getting wet.

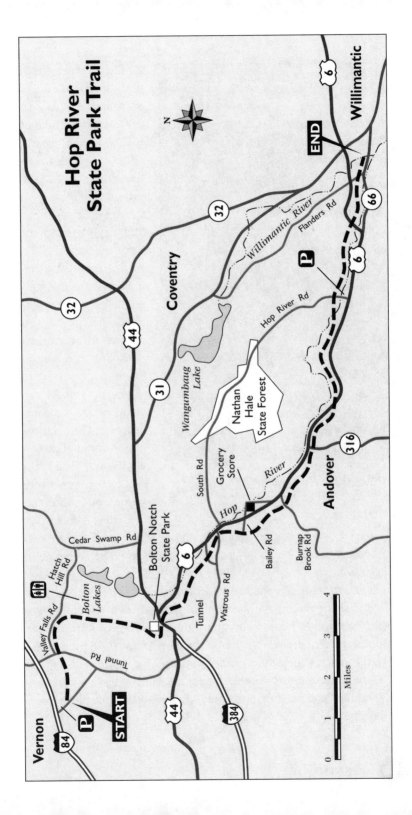

On the other side of the tunnel, the trail is surrounded by towering outcroppings of rock that reach nearly 50 feet high and continue the effect of the tunnel you just passed through. Small birch and maple trees sprout from the jagged cliffs. At this point, Route 6 is just above the trail on the left side and parallels the trail all the way to Willimantic.

Beyond the 5-mile mark, the trail veers right away from Route 6 and makes a steady descent. The trail remains somewhat elevated on a ledge and becomes progressively more wooded for the next mile. Before the 7-mile mark is a yellow gate, signaling an upcoming road. This one is Steel Crossing Road, and a few parking spaces are available here, not far from Route 6.

The Hop River State Park Trail crosses on top of this attractive stone tunnel that gives Tunnel Road its name.

The trail remains wooded and fairly rugged for the next few miles. There are intermittent railroad ties along this stretch. Here, too, you will find mountain bikers who enjoy the challenge of jumping the tree branches that are strewn across the corridor. At the 8-mile mark, the trail crosses Bailey Road and then passes by an old whistle post and some outcroppings of rock. If you are touring the trail on Sunday, you may hear gunfire in the area. Turkey shoots take place many Sundays between 10:00 A.M. and 2:00 P.M.

Soon the trail reaches a short bridge, which is passable. However, if you want to detour around it, get off the trail at Bailey, head left down to Route 6, and turn right. After passing a small plaza with a grocery store, turn left on Aspinall Drive, the trail's next road crossing. You quickly reach another set of yellow gates and a road crossing at Burnap Bridge Road.

This is about the trail's midway point. On the right is a brook, which cascades down a series of rocks and then reappears on the trail's left side. Fir and pine trees are blended with hardwoods in this fragrant area. The surface here is a mix of cinder and gravel. The trail veers toward Route 6 as you make your way to the tiny town of Andover, which is the birthplace of American patriot Nathan Hale. Beyond mile 10 the trail closely parallels the highway with the trail situated atop a retaining wall. At 10.5 miles, the trail reaches Route 316, where a large bridge span is missing. You'll need to go down a relatively steep embankment, cross the road at grade, and head back up on the other side. Much of the attractive stonework that once supported the bridge is still in place. You can also leave the corridor here for a short time. If you take the short, dead-end street just to the left of the corridor, you will see the town hall.

Back on the trail, the views become more mountainous in the distance and the surface gets more bumpy, with occasional railroad ties still in place. A tree farm is on the left as the trail approaches Merritt Valley Road, just beyond the 11-mile mark. This road crossing, where an open bridge span is closed to trail users, signals the beginning of a section of the Hop River Trail that should only be attempted by the adventurous.

Beyond the Merritt Valley Road are five bridges in less than 4 miles. Every bridge has large gaps in its decking and no handrails. If you have no qualms about seeing water rushing below as you carefully make your way across these bridges, then proceed across Merritt Valley Road and continue along the trail. For those with any doubts, cross under the trail corridor and proceed on residential Merritt Valley Road. Homes line the right side of the trail. The trail cuts under Route 6. At the main thoroughfare, in about a half-mile, turn right. Continue on the narrow shoulder for about 2.5 miles and turn left on Hop River Road. In 0.2 mile, the trail reaches a one-lane bridge.

Take a look to the left to see a long wooden trestle—this is the last of the bridges that caused this detour. A parking area and familiar yellow gates are located on the left side of the road.

Turn right to resume the trail or go left for a very short distance to take a look at the biggest bridge you bypassed. It's worth a quick look for the first view you have of the Hop River. On the opposite side of Hop River Road, the trail continues toward Willimantic. The Hop River meanders in and out of view on the right.

The trail is quite rutted in this area, likely the result of dirt bikes being used illegally here. The path passes cornfields on the right and goes through a relatively new concrete culvert. You will pass under some power lines before the trail goes through a quarry about 1.5 miles from Hop River Road.

Soon the trail crosses over a very short bridge, the intriguing decking of which is made of former railroad tracks placed side by side. As the trail approaches the 16.5-mile mark, it crosses under a second concrete culvert before passing an original stone mileage marker. The trail begins undulating again as it passes through a cut in the rocks. Beyond 17 miles, the trail reaches King Road. If you continue straight, you immediately reach a bridge across the Hop River. This bridge is not stable, so detour around it by turning left onto King Road after the stop sign. Veer right to get back onto the trail.

You will pass through a third concrete culvert under Flanders Road as you near the end of the trail. At this point, State Route 66 is above on the right. The trail ends within a half-mile at a massive trestle across the Willimantic River.

While this bridge is not passable, many trail enthusiasts in Connecticut hope one day to open this bridge, which would then allow the Hop River State Park Trail to connect with Airline Trail State Park, making Willimantic the rail-trail hub of eastern Connecticut.

4 Larkin Bridle Path

This little-known gem of a trail offers solitude and sylvan surroundings just off Connecticut's main east-west thoroughfare (I–84).

Activities:

Location: New Haven County

Length: 10.7 miles

Surface: Original ballast and cinder

Wheelchair access: None

Difficulty: Moderate

Food: Southbury has several restaurants and fast-food establishments.

Rest rooms: Hop Brook Lake Recreation Area

Seasons: Open year-round.

Access and parking: From I–84, take exit 15. Turn right and travel south on State Route 67 for 0.5 mile. Turn left just past the tennis courts, which are part of Southbury's Community House Park, to the parking lot. Travel 0.4 mile down Jeremy Swamp Road to the Larkin Bridle Path. The trail's western terminus at Kettletown Road is 0.5 mile to the right. You can head in that direction or begin traveling east. The trail continues eastward for more than 10 miles.

Rentals: The Bike Rack, 1059 Huntington Avenue, Waterbury, CT; (860) 755–0347

Contact: Tim O'Donoghue, Supervisor, Southford Falls State Park, 175 Quaker Farms Road, Southbury, CT 06488-2750; (203) 264–5169.

• •

This Southeastern Connecticut trail takes travelers past forests, ponds, and wetlands in relative isolation. Although the railroad had many owners, it was originally developed by the New York and New England Railroad in the 1880s. The line ran from Waterbury, Connecticut (once home to a thriving brass industry) to Brewster, New York. The line carried both freight and passengers. In 1943, Dr. Charles Larkin purchased the corridor from the New Haven Railroad and donated it to the state for the express purpose of creating a state bridle path. Today, equestrians—as well as walkers, runners, hikers, mountain bicyclists and cross-country skiers—can thank Dr. Larkin for this quiet stretch of wilderness.

The beginning of the trail feels quite isolated, even though it is only a short distance from the interstate. Trees meet overhead and only an occasional house interrupts the trail's sylvan surroundings. Curt Smith Road crosses the trail a little more than a mile from Kettletown Road, followed shortly by Route 67. The trail for the next mile is quite wide and still shrouded with trees.

The path passes a small pond before crossing State Route 188 near the 2.5-mile mark. The Southbury Fire Station is located here, and there is parking for several cars. Within a half-mile, the trail passes some wetlands and a creek off to the left. The trail ascends steadily at this point while crossing Eight Mile Creek and Pope Road. The crossing at Hawley Road is preceded by a short and narrow uphill stretch—most likely a bridge was removed here.

Just before the 4-mile mark, the trail crosses over some railroad ties, the first sign of the corridor's previous use. The path begins to widen at this point. There are few homes here, although the small Waterbury-Oxford Airport is nearby. After crossing Christian

Road, the surface is a more hard-packed cinder and the vegetation is a bit sparser. At times you will get views of rolling hills on the left and an expansive meadow on the right.

Beyond 5.5. miles, the trail passes through a

Lined with wetlands and wildflowers, Towantic Pond is one of the most scenic spots along the trail.

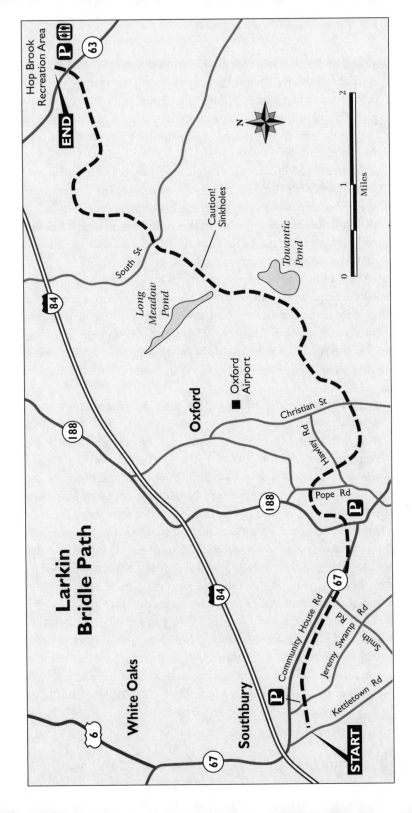

Larkin
Bridle Path

Hop Brook Recreation Area

63

END

N

Caution! Sinkholes

South St

Long Meadow Pond

Towantic Pond

84

Oxford

Oxford Airport

Christian St

188

Hawley Rd

Pope Rd

P

188

67

P

Community House Rd

Jeremy Swamp Rd

Smith Rd

Kettletown Rd

START

White Oaks

Southbury

6

67

84

188

Miles

0   1   2

significant rock cut, where the path narrows. Soon the path leads to Towantic Pond, one of the prettiest spots along the trail.

As the trail continues, it begins to go uphill, followed by a steep and rocky downhill before crossing the next road at 6.5 miles. The next half-mile of trail is sunk between steep rock cuts and is typically wet and muddy.

At the next road crossing a cryptic sign instructs equestrians to walk their horses for the next mile because of possible danger from sinkholes. Accidents have occurred in this area, so heed the warning. The trail descends somewhat in this mile-long section, although it is still high above most of its surroundings. The trail passes several rocky outcropping over the next few miles.

At the 8-mile mark, the trail reaches South Street, where it is possible to see much of the original stone foundation of a railroad bridge long since removed. With the bridge missing, it is necessary to go down and back up to cross the road. On the opposite side, the trail continues to the right of what appears to be a fork. This stretch of trail is densely wooded and the trail surface is a bit sandy.

Soon the trail enters an extensive rock cut where trees tower overhead and ferns seem to grow straight out of the rocks. This area has a shadowy, jungle-like look and the temperature is significantly cooler than the rest of the trail during the summer months. It is a nice place to stop and relax for a few minutes. After another road crossing, the trail is again surrounded by woods and you feel as if you are in the middle of the wilderness.

The trail remains high on a ridge as it passes the 9.5-mile mark. Here it traverses more wetlands and a view of rolling hills in the distance. As you approach mile 10 you pass several homes, followed by a town-home development. The trail becomes quite rocky and for the first time civilization's less attractive qualities are visible, with trash strewn along the trail corridor. Next, you see busy Route 63 below you. A bridge has been removed here so you will have to cross the road to continue—use caution.

The trail officially ends on the opposite side of Route 63 at Hop Brook Lake, where there is a recreation area controlled by the

Army Corps of Engineers. To enter the recreation area, turn left on Route 63 and travel a half-mile; the main entrance is on the right. Picnic facilities and a swimming area are available at this site, which is open to the public from mid-April through the end of October.

You will pass through many extensive rock cuts along the Larkin Bridle Path.

Starting high on a ridge and then descending into a steep ravine, this trail has a sense of being far away from the real world, yet it is only minutes from the suburban town of Vernon.

Activities:

Location: Tolland County

Length: 3.5 miles

Surface: Packed dirt

Wheelchair access: Yes

Difficulty: Easy

Food: Restaurants are available in the town of Vernon.

Rest rooms: Portable toilets are available at the parking lot.

Seasons: Open year-round.

Access and parking: From Route 84, take exit 65 and proceed east. After about 0.25 mile, on the right, is a Kentucky Fried Chicken restaurant. Take a right after the restaurant onto Dobson Road. Go 3 blocks and turn left onto Church Street. The parking lot is on the left.

Rentals:

- The Bike Shop, 681 Main Street, Manchester, CT; (860) 647–1027.
- The Cycle Center, 30 Post Road Plaza, Vernon, CT; (860) 872–7740.

Contact: Bruce Dinnie, Vernon Parks and Recreation, 120 South Street, Vernon, CT 06066-4404; (860) 872–6118.

This pleasant rail-trail offers a relatively easy trip through light forest on top of a ridge. It's a perfect trail for families with young children, or for anyone out for a pleasant walk in the woods.

The Hartford, Providence, and Fishkill Railroad began operation of the Rockville Railroad in 1863. In 1878 it became part of the New York and New England Railroad and twenty years later was sold to the New York, New Haven, and Hartford Railroad. In 1907 the line was electrified and trolleys operated over the line until the 1920s. Passenger service ended in 1929.

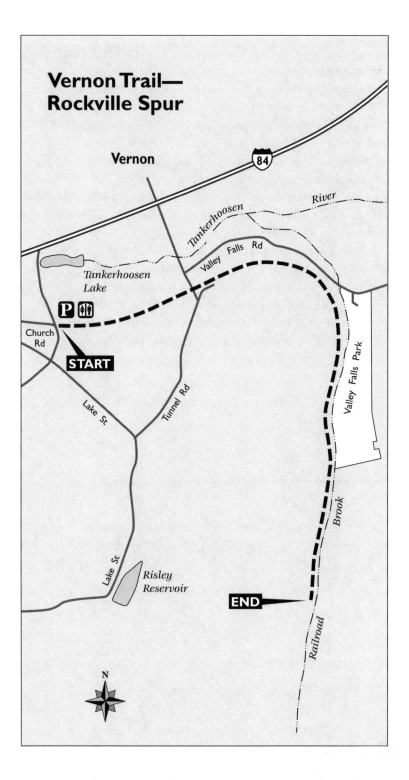

As you begin the trail at the parking lot, go slowly because there is a road crossing almost immediately after the trail begins. Once on the other side of the road, the trail immediately begins its traverse along the top of a ridge. A pleasant residential community can be viewed on the right, with backyards in view from the trail. The ridge continues for an additional half-mile. At 0.9 mile, the path crosses a small bridge. A road can be seen on the right about 100 feet below the trail. More houses come into view on the right at the 1-mile point. After this, however, the path quickly passes into a young forest of birch trees. At 1.8 miles, rock formations line the right side of the path while the hill slopes downward on the left.

At 2.6 miles, the forest becomes more dense, but the path becomes sandier after 3.0 miles. At 3.2 miles, old railroad ties line the left side of the trail. A small waterfall can be viewed at 3.4 miles. At 3.5 miles is a turnaround area on the left. From this point on, the trail is less well maintained although it continues into Rockville, a town once known for its mills and now a quiet, suburban town.

MORE RAIL-TRAILS

(A) Airline State Park Trail (North)

The Airline State Park Trail North is a work in progress. It currently extends for 26 miles through northeastern Connecticut.

Activities:

Location: Windham County

Length: 26 miles

Surface: Portions of the trail are paved at the beginning; original ballast thereafter.

Wheelchair access: No

Difficulty: Difficult

Food: There are restaurants and convenience stores along Route 16.

Rest rooms: None

Seasons: Open year-round.

Access and parking: The trail can be reached at the Goodwin State Forest Conservation Center on Potter Road on Route 6 in Hampton. It can also be accessed from the Route 66 and Route 6 interchange.

Rentals:
- Rainbow Cycle, 385 Valley Street, Willimantic, CT; (860) 423–7182.
- Scott's Cyclery, 1171 Main Street, Willimantic, CT; (860) 423–8889.

Contact: John Folsom, Park Supervisor, Connecticut Department of Environmental Protection; (860) 928–6121

· · · · · · · · · · · · · · · · · · · ·

The Airline Railroad was given its name as the most expedient route to and from Boston and New York in the late nineteenth century. Between 1891 and 1895 the famous "White Train" used this line. The Boston–New York line was in full operation until 1924. Passenger service was completely discontinued in 1937.

This trail is an extension of the Airline State Park Trail (South). It now extends from Windham to Putnam. The most scenic portion of the trail can be reached by starting at the Goodwin State Forest

Conservation Center. The trail runs northward through Beaver Brook State Park and past the Hamden Reservoir. The trail ends at the Massachusetts border but will eventually connect with a trail in the Douglas State Forest in Massachusetts. The National Guard is developing the trail in both states.

B Farmington River Trail/Punch Brook Access Area

This trail is a work in progress. Following the Farmington River, it's an easy bike ride with some nice views of the river.

Activities:

Location: Hartford County

Length: When completed the trail will be 16 miles in length.

Surface: Dirt

Wheelchair access: Yes

Difficulty: Easy

Food: There are restaurants and food stores in the towns of Unionville, Collinsville, Canton, and Simsbury.

Rest rooms: Rest rooms are available at Stratton State Park in Simsbury.

Seasons: Open year-round.

Access and parking: From Hartford, travel west on Route 6 until it intersects with Route 4 at exit 39. The trail parallels Route 4 for several miles before following Route 179 to Collinsville. There are several parking areas along the way. At Route 4, parking is available at Quirk Park and at the the intersections of Route 4 and 179. There is also parking in Collinsville.

Rentals:
- Alpine Ski Works, 1064 South Main Street, Cheshire, CT; (860) 272–6614.
- The Bike Rack, 1650 Whitney Avenue, Hamden, CT; (860) 281–6660.

Transportation:
- Dattco, Inc., 20 Industrial Drive, Avon, CT; (860) 673–7231.
- Rainbow Bus Lines, Inc., 825 Bloomfield Avenue, Windsor, CT; (860) 688–1841.
- M + J Bus Line, 535 Salmon Brook Street, Granby, CT; (860) 653–0627.

Contact: William Mattioli, Water Safety Coordinator, State Parks Division, State of Connecticut Department of Environmental Protection, Hartford, CT 06106-5127; (860) 424–3209; fax (860) 424–4070; http://dep.state.ct.us/.

The Farmington River is the central theme of this trail, which follows the river from Farmington to Collinsville. The riparian woodlands along the trail are especially lush during the spring and summer months. After Collinsville, the trail travels eastward past the Roaring Brook Nature Center and Massacoe State Forest and Stratton Brook State Forest.

The Farmington River Trail follows two separate rail lines. From Farmington to Collinsville, the rail line was built by the New Haven & Northampton Railroad in 1850 and traveled for 8 miles. The line was extended to Pine Meadow in 1855 and to New Hartford in 1876. It was bought by the New Haven Railroad in 1887. Passenger service was discontinued in 1928. The section from Collinsville to Simsbury was built by the Connecticut Western Railroad in 1871. It was also assumed by the New Haven Railroad in 1927. Although passenger service ended once the railroad changed hands, freight service continued until 1932.

Flowers adorn this 1892 bridge along the Farmington River Trail.

Picture-postcard perfect and very isolated, this short trail is a delightful rural retreat.

Activities:

Location: Windham County

Length: 3 miles

Surface: Dirt

Wheelchair access: No

Difficulty: Moderate

Food: There are restaurants and convenience stores in Moosup and Sterling.

Rest rooms: None

Seasons: Open year-round.

Access and parking: From Providence follow Route 6 west to I–395. Take exit 89 (Route 14) east to Moosup. Follow the highway through the center of Moosup. Parking is available on the left, near the Moosup Adult Learning Center.

Rentals: None

Contact: Scott Dawley, Pachaug State Forest Headquarters; (860) 376–4075.

• • • • • • • • • • • • • • • • • • • •

The Moosup-Sterling line was once part of the Hartford, Providence, and Fishkill Railroad and opened in 1854. About a year after it was built, the line spanned 122 miles, from Providence to Waterbury. The New York & New England Railroad bought the railroad in 1878. Twenty years later it was absorbed by the New York, New Haven & Hartford

Water cascades over the dam on Moosup River.

A bridge on the Moosup Trail.

Railroad. Passenger service continued until 1931. The line was abandoned in 1967.

Equally bucolic and scenic, the trail feels like it is miles away from civilization. The two small towns that are connected by the trail, Moosup and Sterling, have a true rural quality to them. The trail parallels the Moosup River. Several bridges on the trail are worthy of note. You cross the first bridge at the beginning of the trail in Moosup. After another mile, a second bridge can be viewed to the left of the trail. Take a moment to enjoy the view: The river has been dammed here, creating a waterfall that cascades into the river below. The trail becomes more rural for the next couple of miles, coursing through a light forest. A quarry can be viewed on the right at about the 2-mile mark. The trail continues past Sterling; however, this part is not well maintained. Plans for the future include continuing the trail to the Rhode Island border and continuing through the neighboring state.

This short trail pays homage to Connecticut's railroad history and the history of the town of Putnam with a series of exhibits along the path.

Activities:

Location: Windham County

Length: 2 miles

Surface: Bituminous concrete and asphalt

Wheelchair access: Yes

Difficulty: Easy

Food: Restaurants are available in Putnam.

Rest rooms: Rest rooms should be available in Putnam.

Seasons: Open year-round.

Access and parking: From I–395 southbound, take exit 97 and follow Route 44 west. Take a left onto Kennedy Drive. A parking lot is situated on the right just after Bridge Street. From I–395 northbound, take exit 95 and turn right at the end of the ramp onto Kennedy Drive. There are several parking lots about 0.5 mile up the road on the left.

Rentals:
- Bolio Sporting Goods, 131 Main Street, Webster, MA; (508) 943–8007.
- On Target Sports, 89 Main Street, Harrisville, RI; (401) 567–0780.

Contact: Director, Economic Development Commission, 112 Main Street, Putnam, CT 06260; (860) 963–6811.

• • • • • • • • • • • • • • • • • • • •

The short but sweet Putnam River Trail follows the eastern shore of the Quinebaug River. It passes through woodlands, several parks, and through Putnam's downtown antique shopping district. Several revitalized mills can be seen along the way. The trail pays tribute to Putnam's railroad history, its textile mills, and its founding citizens in the five historic exhibits located along the trail. The great flood of 1955 is also highlighted. Take note of the four bridges adjacent to the trail, including a 200-foot-long pedestrian bridge built on the stone foundation of an old railroad trestle.

The Boston, Hartford & Erie Railroad built this segment of the

Boston to Hartford line in 1872. It was bought by the New York &
New England Railroad in 1875 and later purchased by the New Haven
Railroad in 1898. In August 1955, a terrible flood destroyed a bridge
near Putnam, bringing an end to service on this line.

(E) Stratton Brook State Park

This short trail is perfect for bicyclists, joggers, and walkers as it
passes through Stratton Brook State Park.

Activities:

Location: Hartford County

Length: 3 miles

Surface: Dirt

Wheelchair access: Yes

Difficulty: Easy

Food: Simsbury has all kinds of restaurants, from plain to fancy.

Rest rooms: There are rest rooms at Stratton Brook State Park.

Seasons: Open year-round.

Access and parking: From I–91, take a left onto Route 20. Take a left onto
Route 10. Once you have entered the town of Simsbury, watch for the First
Church of Christ on the right. Turn right onto West Street. In about 1 mile,
you will pass Simsbury High School, on the right. The entrance to Stratton
State Park is about 0.25 mile past the high school, on the left.

Rentals: Bicycle Cellar, 532 Hopmeadow Street, Simsbury, CT; (860) 658–1311.

Transportation:
• Dattco, Inc., 20 Industrial Drive, Avon, CT; (860) 673–7231.
• Rainbow Bus Lines Inc, 825 Bloomfield Avenue, Windsor, CT; (860)
  688–1841.
• M + J Bus Line, 535 Salmon Brook Street, Granby, CT; (860) 653–0627.

Contact: Dan Dickinson, Supervisor, Stratton Brook State Park; (860) 242–1158.

• •

The Stratton Brook rail-trail begins at the covered bridge in Stratton
Brook State Park. You can take the trail eastward for 1 mile as the
trail plays hide-and-seek with Stratton Brook. The remains of an old
rail bridge can be viewed from the trail about 150 feet from the trail-

head. Traveling west, you can follow the trail for 2 miles. Stratton Brook is never far away. The trail passes by wetlands at 0.6 mile and woods at 1.2 miles.

The Connecticut Western Railroad opened this line in 1871. It became part of the Central New England Railway in 1898. It was later taken over by the New Haven Railroad in 1927. Passenger service was discontinued and the line was closed in 1932.

Future Connecticut Rail-Trails

Connecticut has a number of rail-trail projects in the works. The Farmington Canal and Farmington River Trails will continue to be developed and upon completion will be called the Farmington Canal Heritage Trail. A segment from Avon to Plainfield will be added to the Farmington Canal Linear State Park Trail and will add 8.3 miles to that rail-trail, and an additional link between Cheshire and Southington will add another 9.5 miles. Once completed, the new Farmington Canal Heritage Trail will run from New Haven to the Massachusetts border, a total of 66 miles.

Other projects include a Bridgeport to Newtown to Trumbull trail. This will also include a spur as part of the Pequonnock River Greenway. The length of the trail is unknown at this time.

The towns of Derby, Manchester, and East Hampton are planning to develop a rail-trail. A rail-trail along the Old Connecticut and Western Railroad is also in the planning stage. We can also look forward to the Wethersfield and Rocky Hills Paths and Wethersfield Secondary Line rail-trails.

For more information about the projected trails, check out the Connecticut state government Web page at www.state.ct.us.

Rails-to-Trails

MAINE

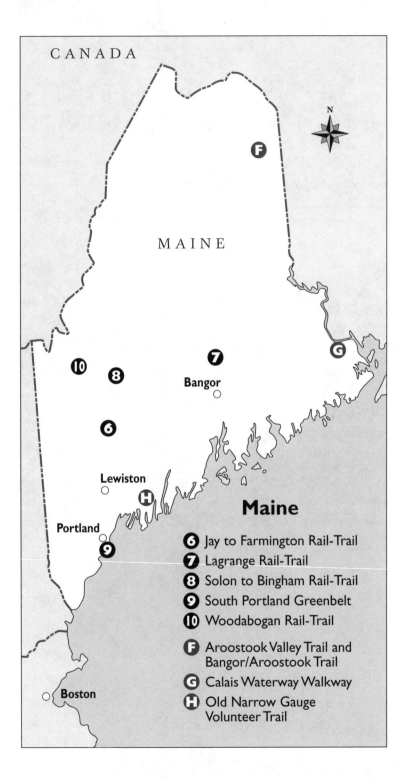

CANADA

MAINE

N

F

10 **8** **7**
Bangor
○

G

6

Lewiston
○

H

Portland
○
9

Boston
○

Maine

6 Jay to Farmington Rail-Trail
7 Lagrange Rail-Trail
8 Solon to Bingham Rail-Trail
9 South Portland Greenbelt
10 Woodabogan Rail-Trail

F Aroostook Valley Trail and
Bangor/Aroostook Trail
G Calais Waterway Walkway
H Old Narrow Gauge
Volunteer Trail

INTRODUCTION

Maine is vast and beautiful. The largest state in New England, it spans 300 miles from north to south and 200 miles from east to west. Its coastline is famous for its breathtaking beauty. The York County coast region encompasses the southern coastal resort towns of York, Ogunquit, and Kennebunkport. The latter was the summer home of President George Bush during his presidency.

Portland is a lovely city with beautiful old homes and a recently renovated downtown area. The Old Port Exchange, one of the best urban renovation projects on the East Coast, gives downtown Portland a wonderful sense of history and style. Along cobblestone streets are restaurants, jazz clubs, and boutiques.

Up the coast from Portland is Maine's Midcoast region, anchored by Penobscot Bay. Residents of this area are fierce loyalists and claim that this is the part of the Maine Coast that has preserved much of its original flavor. Farther north is Acadia National Park with 40,000 acres of woods and mountains.

Much of inland Maine is quite remote. The northern portion of the state is almost uninhabited. Farmland dots the landscape. Many of the towns in the region consist of a market, gasoline station, and post office, all rolled into one.

Maine has fourteen rail-trails covering 413 miles. Near Portland is the South Portland Greenway, which offers wonderful views of the city's skyline. To the north are more remote rail-trails, such as the Jay to Farmington Trail and the Lagrange Trail. Here you will find trails bordering rivers and traversing through farmland, marshes, and forests. Farther north yet, toward the Canadian border, is the 71-mile-long Aroostook Rail-Trail, resplendent in its remote beauty.

An additional thirteen rail-trails are currently projected for the state.

Maine's

TOP RAIL-TRAILS

6 | Jay to Farmington Rail-Trail

Developed primarily as a route for snowmobiles and off-road vehicle enthusiasts, the Jay to Farmington Trail also appeals to the hiker and mountain bicyclist with a rugged spirit.

Activities:

Location: Franklin County

Length: 14.5 miles

Surface: Gravel, sand, and cinder

Wheelchair access: No

Difficulty: Moderate. A sandy surface makes this trail rather difficult to travel by bicycle, even with fat-tired mountain bikes. This trail is best for hiking, horseback riding, and for winter sports, such as cross-country skiing, snowshoeing, and snowmobiling.

Food: Restaurants are available in Jay, Wilton, and Farmington.

Rest rooms: None at the trail, but rest rooms should be available in Jay, Wilton, and Farmington.

Seasons: Open year-round.

Access and parking: From Jay, take Route 4 north nearly 35 miles from I–495 through the town of Livermore Falls. At 0.5 mile past the Town of Jay Municipal Building, turn left onto Old Jay Road and go past the Knights of Columbus building. Beyond an auto body shop, there is a small park where parking is available. To get to the trailhead, return to Old Jay Road and take a left. The trail begins on the left about 150 feet up the road.

Rentals: Northern Lights, 2 Front Street, Farmington, ME; (207) 778–6566.

Contact: Scott Ramsey, Supervisor, Off Road Vehicles, Bureau of Parks and Recreation, Department of Conservation, Station #22, Augusta, ME 04333-0022; (207) 287–3821; fax (207) 287–4956.

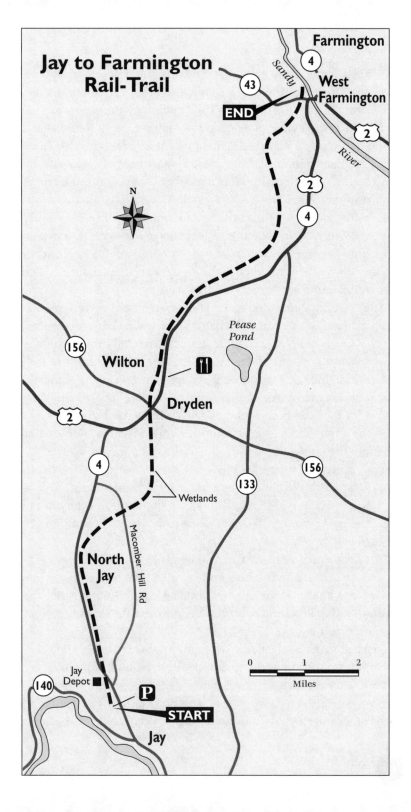

T his is Maine at its most rural and unspoiled. It's not for everyone, however; the trail's sandy and often rutted surface demands your attention. Take your time and enjoy the scenery.

This line originally belonged to the Maine Central Railroad and served many manufacturing plants in the area. The corridor came under the management of the Maine Department of Conservation in 1982, after snowmobile riders around the state showed a strong interest in the corridor.

Heading north on the trail, the surroundings are pleasantly wooded. Within a half-mile the path comes to the Jay Depot, which today houses some small businesses. Immediately past the depot the trail crosses well-traveled Route 4 at grade, so use caution. The wide trail is quite sandy in this early section.

After passing a pond and several homes, the trail begins to ascend on a rutted and sandy surface, which can be quite taxing for cyclists. The trail levels out past the 2-mile mark and overall the trail surface improves at this point. The surroundings are marshy and the wetland views to the right are particularly appealing. Bring mosquito repellent during the warmer months; the wetlands here are a breeding ground for the little pests and they are abundant in the area.

At the 4-mile mark, the trail closely parallels Route 4. Mountains dominate the landscape to the left. On the right is a massive retaining wall composed of granite blocks. Formerly the site of the North Jay rail yard, this wall lines the corridor for several hundred feet. A picnic table sits in a clearing, still within the border of the old rail yard. The trail resumes an uphill climb as it passes the community of North Jay.

The surface in this segment is intermittently hard-packed cinder and soft sand. The fragrant smell of pine lingers in the air while aspen trees quake at the slightest breeze. Still climbing, the trail crosses Old Jay Road and soon two steeples and the town's rooftops are visible below.

Just before the 5-mile mark, the path crosses Macomber Hill Road, where pine and fir trees dominate the route on both sides of a long rock cut. Mosses and ferns cover much of the craggy rock, while pine trees grow over the rock formation. The surface turns to a deep sand on the other side of the cut, although the splendid forest setting helps

The path is quite sandy—but nonetheless pretty.

keep your mind off the surface. Looking around at the nearby mountains, which earlier seemed to tower high above, you'll realize how high you've climbed.

The trail again cuts through wetlands beyond the 6-mile mark. Much of this marsh has been created by extensive beaver activity in the area. Beyond the 7.5-mile mark, the trail crosses the four-lane Route 4 (also Route 2) at grade in the town of Wilton, followed shortly by Route 156. Wilton is the trail's midpoint and one of the few places to stop before Farmington. Here you will find a gas station and a couple of small establishments offering limited food and supplies.

If you happen to see a sign saying NO TRESPASSING WITHOUT A PERMIT, don't worry; the sign is aimed only at the automobile that once used the route. The trail narrows for a stretch beyond Wilton and the surface deteriorates into rutted sand. A bridge soon carries you across Wilson Stream, which ripples next to the trail by Route 9. Route 4 continues along the right side for a couple of miles. Just before mile 10 there is a short stretch of hard-packed cinder—a welcome respite from the sand.

Beyond mile 10 is a bridge that passes over Cemetery Street and Wilson Stream. Built by the Western Maine ATV Association and Woodland Wanderers Snowmobile Club, this bridge is designed for one-way snowmobile or off-road vehicle traffic. Use caution on the bridge if other trail users are nearby. The bridge offers sweeping views of the surrounding landscape, including a view of a waterfall on Wilson Stream, to the left. A pizza restaurant is adjacent to the trail just beyond the bridge—the last stop before Farmington.

After the 11-mile mark, the trail passes through a dense pine forest mixed with aspen and oak. The path may seem remote, but civilization is close by on Route 4. At times you will see small signs for shops and restaurants, provided for the benefit of snowmobilers.

The next couple of miles are again remote and wooded. The surface has some rough spots at it passes through wetlands near mile 13.

Beyond mile 14, the trail crosses Hardy Stream over the trail's second-longest bridge. West Farmington can be seen in the distance. Within a half-mile, the trail reaches Route 43, after passing an old oil company building that was once served by the railroad. The trail ends a half-mile farther at Sandy River. This is a peaceful place to stop and rest before venturing into Farmington.

Home to a campus of the University of Maine, Farmington is well worth an extension to your journey of another mile or so. The town is friendly and its Victorian architecture is quite enchanting. To get into town, go back to Route 43, turn left and almost immediately see signs for Routes 4 and 2. Turn left onto the state routes and continue another mile to Main Street. Downtown is on the left and offers restaurants, shops, banks, a bike shop, and an ice cream shop. The university is to the right.

Treetops touch and create a verdant tunnel.

7 Lagrange Rail-Trail

This rail-trail takes its guests through a delightful stretch of rural Maine not often seen by tourists. The trestle bridge at the end of the trail is particularly noteworthy.

Activities:

Location: Piscataquis and Penobscot Counties

Length: 12 miles

Surface: Packed gravel

Wheelchair access: No

Difficulty: Moderate

Food: A small convenience store is located in Lagrange.

Rest rooms: None

Seasons: Open year-round.

Access and parking: From I–95, take a left onto Route 16 north to South Lagrange. SOUTH LAGRANGE is literally marked on the side of a house on the left side of the road, about 7 miles from I–95. A small parking lot is provided at the end of a dirt lane; the lane and lot are just past the house and are well marked.

Rentals: None

Contact: Scott Ramsey, Supervisor, Off Road Vehicles, Bureau of Parks and Recreation, Department of Conservation, Station #22, Augusta, ME 04333-0022; (207) 287–3821; fax (207) 287–4956.

• •

The Bangor and Aroostook Railroad opened this 28-mile-long line in 1907 and provided passenger service until 1930. The line was abandoned in 1977.

From the parking lot, proceed north; the trail begins immediately. At 0.2 mile, the trail goes under a Bangor and Aroostook Railroad overpass and then narrows after passing a brightly painted orange metal gate. Soon a pond comes into view on the left. The trail passes through farmland and meadows before reaching another crossing at 1.9 miles. For the next mile, the trail takes you through a forest of pine and birch. At 3.8 miles the trail become densely wooded on both sides. At 4.4 miles, the path crosses a paved town road, followed by a second crossing at Route 155. Use caution at these crossings—the traffic moves quickly.

For the next couple of miles, the path traverses farmland and light forest, opening up to a marsh on the left at 5.7 miles. There are road crossings at 7.2 miles and 8.0 miles as Medford Road crisscrosses the path. Again, caution is advised.

At 8.4 miles, the trail crosses Cold Stream on a small wooden bridge with metal siding. The landscape begins to open up at 9.0 miles as the trail approaches farmland, which dominates the landscape by the time you reach the 10-mile mark. The trail becomes tougher after this; a rocky and rutted surface and a sharp upgrade at 10.2 miles make tough going for cyclists. At 10.4 miles, the trail proceeds downhill and crosses a small creek before heading uphill again. There are road crossings at 11.2 miles; at 11.7 miles, Medford Road once again crosses the trail. The trail turns left and then sharply right before joining with a gravel road. It ends shortly after this point at the trestle bridge crossing the Piscataquis River. The little village of Medford (consisting solely of a small town hall and a church) is a short way back along the Medford Road, heading southward.

The trestle bridge at the end of the trail crosses the Piscataquis River.

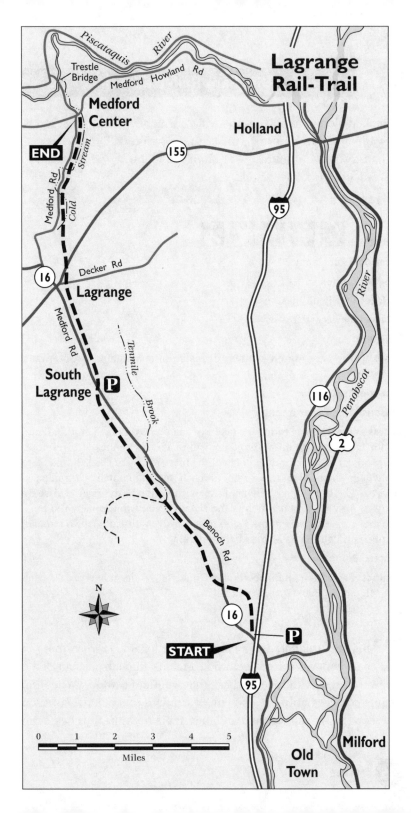

Lagrange
Rail-Trail

Piscataquis River

Trestle Bridge

Medford Howland Rd

Medford Center

Holland

END

155

95

Medford Rd

Cold Stream

16

Decker Rd

Lagrange

Medford Rd

River

South Lagrange

P

Tenmile Brook

116

Penobscot

2

Benoch Rd

N

16

START

P

95

Old Town

Milford

0   1   2   3   4   5
Miles

8 Solon to Bingham Rail-Trail

Tucked along the edge of the wide Kennebec River, the Solon to Bingham Trail offers a pleasant diversion from I–95. Less than forty-five minutes away from the highway, this flat and scenic trail is family-friendly.

Activities:

Location: Somerset County

Length: 7 miles

Surface: Crushed limestone

Wheelchair access: No

Difficulty: Easy

Food: There is a limited number of restaurants available in Solon and Bingham.

Rest rooms: None

Seasons: Open year-round.

Access and parking: From I–95, take exit 36 and travel north on U.S. Route 201 for more than 20 miles into Solon. To reach the trailhead, turn left on Fall Road, an eighth of a mile north of the intersection of U.S. 201 and State Route 8; go downhill and veer right to reach the boat launch and trail parking area. The trail, which seems like a continuation of the road, will be directly in front of you, paralleling the river. (If you want to view the huge dam that creates the Caratunk Falls and a massive railroad trestle overhead, continue straight on Falls Road before parking.)

Rentals: None

Contact: Roger Polin, Kennebec Valley Trails, 248 Madison Avenue, Skowhegan, ME 04976-1306; (207) 474–5151.

• •

This line originated as a narrow-gauge logging railroad that ran between Anson and Rockwood, Maine, although portions of the line were used by tourists early in the twentieth century. When the logging ceased, Central Maine Power acquired much of the corridor. In recent years the Kennebec Valley Rails organization has been

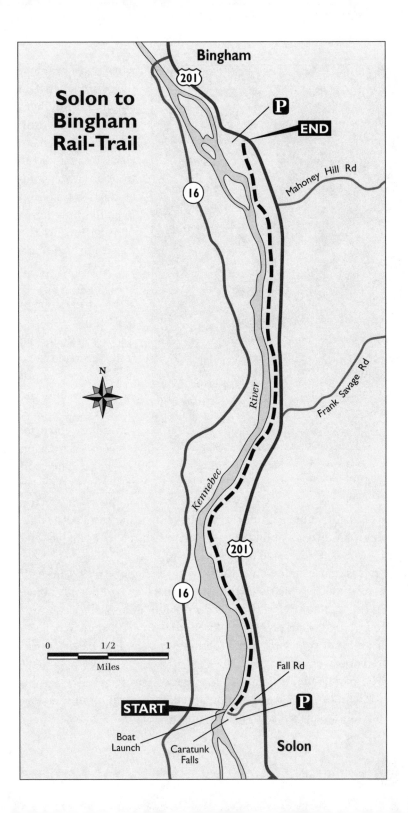

Solon to Bingham Rail-Trail

Bingham

201

16

P

END

Mahoney Hill Rd

Frank Savage Rd

River

Kennebec

201

16

N

0   1/2   1
Miles

Fall Rd

START

P

Boat
Launch

Caratunk
Falls

Solon

A man and his dog along the Solon to Bingham Rail-Trail.

working to promote the corridor between Solon and Bingham as a multiuse trail. The group's ultimate goal is to create a continuous water-and-land-based trail from Belgrade (just north of Augusta) to the Canadian border. Currently, the Solon to Bingham Rail-Trail is the cornerstone of that effort.

As you begin the trail, the wide Kennebec River captivates you—and the smooth surface of the path allows you to focus your attention on the river. The trail carves along the edge of the river for the first 2 miles. Mountain bluffs rise along the river's western edge while a mix of hardwoods and softwoods—aspen, birch, oak, maple, and pine—lines the right side of the trail.

In less than a mile Route 201 runs parallel to the trail. The path sinks down next to the river while the highway is significantly above on the right. Soon the trail takes on the feel of an island, as water surrounds both sides of the path for more than a half-mile. When the river and trail veer away from the highway, the trail passes a residential enclave.

The path remains deep in the gorge of the river valley for the next few miles. The views are breathtaking. Traveling in this area during fall foliage season—or anytime near sunset—makes for an even more memorable journey. The mountains seem to rise straight up from the river's edge, creating a wonderful reflection in the Kennebec River, especially in the morning and evening.

By the time the trail reaches the 4.5-mile mark, a thin band of trees begins to separate the path from the river. In less than 2 miles, the trail veers more to the right—away from the river—eventually turning toward U.S. Route 201. A small footbridge signals the trail's end. You soon reach Route 201. If you're in the mood for more adventure, turn left and head down the highway until you reach the whitewater-rafting information center.

The Kennebec River's presence defines this rail-trail.

9   South Portland Greenbelt

This short trail offers a trip through South Portland with spectacular views of the Portland skyline. A favorite for locals, it also offers tourists a chance to see the city at its best.

Activities:

Location: Cumberland County

Length: 3.5 miles

Surface: Asphalt

Wheelchair access: Limited

Difficulty: Easy

Food: Restaurants are available on Broadway and at the Route 77 intersection.

Rest rooms: None

Seasons: Open year-round.

Access and parking: From I–95, take exit 7. After the toll booth, take the second right onto Broadway. Within 2 miles you cross Route 1; be sure to continue straight on Broadway. In just over 1 mile, turn left onto Elm Street. Take a right onto Pearl Street. The trail begins on the right at the end of Pearl Street. There is no designated parking, so find a legal space on one of the side streets, or park on Broadway, near Elm.

Rentals: Joe Jones Sports, 456 Payne Road, Scarborough, ME; (207) 885–5635.

Transportation: South Portland Bus Service; (207) 767–5556.

Contact: Charles Hauser, Planning Director, City Hall, 25 Cottage Road, South Portland, ME 04106-3604; (207) 767–7602; fax (207) 767–7620; e-mail: tex@ime.net.

• •

A cross the harbor from downtown Portland, this tiny gem of a trail offers stunning views of Maine's largest city while providing a flavor of the water-based industries that fuel this historic New England port.

The South Portland Greenbelt began as part of a short-line railroad, the Portland Terminal Company. It primarily served the oil industry, which had numerous oil storage tanks lining the waterways

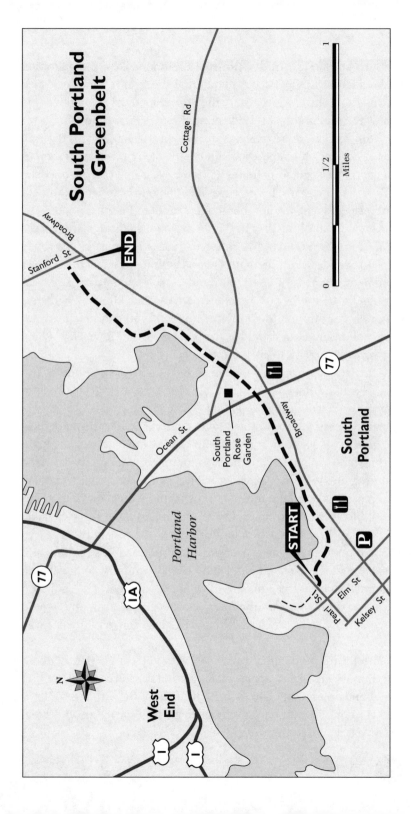

of South Portland. Guilford Transportation took over the operation in the early 1980s but soon abandoned the line in favor of transporting the oil by truck. The city then developed the abandoned line as a waterfront greenway, dedicating the first 2 miles in 1989.

From the end of Pearl Street, turn right. (If you go left, the trail ends at a set of railroad tracks within a couple of blocks.) As soon as you get on the asphalt path, the Portland West End (on the opposite bank of the Fore River) becomes visible. The trail here is popular with local residents who use it for both recreation and transportation.

After less than a half-mile, the trail crosses a bridge and passes the local fire station. Several shopping plazas are located near busy Hanson Street, which the path crosses at grade. This is the start of the downtown area of South Portland, which encompasses several city blocks. In another 0.3 mile, the path reaches Route 77, which is Ocean Street through town. By turning left, you can reach several shops and restaurants, as well as the Post Office and Town Hall. Route 77 also will take you to Portland Harbor.

After the trail crosses Ocean Street, it skirts the edge of the South Portland Rose Garden, which sports roses of every imaginable color, as well as a gazebo and a large fountain.

After crossing busy Cottage Road at grade, where a trail dedication marker is located, the views to the left open up again, highlighting the Portland skyline. This panorama is particularly dramatic at sunset. To the right is a residential neighborhood. After two quick road crossings, the land to the left turns into a meadow with colorful wildflowers. A baseball field lies adjacent to the trail's right side.

The path briefly takes you onto Maple Road at 1.7 miles. The surface is bumpy in this area because of the railroad ties that are still in place under the pavement. There is a community center with a basketball court at the 2-mile mark at Stanford Street. The trail then takes you through a suburban neighborhood until trail end, where a large fence blocks any farther travel because active railroad tracks are still in place.

The future holds great promise for the South Portland Greenbelt. Funding has been approved for a 2-mile eastern extension that would end up at "Bug Light"—the lighthouse at the entrance of Portland Harbor. City planners also hope to get funding for an additional 3-mile extension to the west.

TRAVELS WITH CYNTHIA

by Bruce Emerson

The best part of traveling and taking a vacation is getting away from job pressures. Working as a day trader in the stock market, I rarely leave my computer screen. So, when Cynthia Mascott asked me to join her while she did her research for the Rails-to-Trails Conservancy guidebook, I jumped at the chance to leave the hustle and bustle of life in Los Angeles. I definitely needed time to relax and to leave the stress of work behind me long enough to recharge my batteries.

The first stop on our trip was in Portland, Maine, for the South Portland Greenbelt. Coming from Los Angeles, this was the perfect trail for me to begin our bicycle journey because it offered a perfect mixture of urban and suburban scenery. With its view of the Portland skyline, I felt like I was slowly leaving my urban existence behind without feeling like I was going cold turkey. In addition to scenic beauty, Portland also had clear cell phone reception. With cell phone firmly attached to my belt, I felt secure enough to venture past the city limits. However, I was caught off guard when my cell phone actually began to ring. It took me a moment to figure out what to do. While fumbling for my phone, I saw a local woman walking towards me on the trail. She was carrying grocery bags. She looked up at me with an incredulous look on her face and said aloud and in apparent amazement, "Geesh! Now I've seen everything!" I felt as if I had just been busted, and in my embarrassment and shame, I dropped my phone. Although my cell phone survived the fall, it didn't feel the same when I picked it up. It had become a monkey on my back. This incident served as my "wake up call," and I decided to take a real vacation and to leave the cell phone in my suitcase.

One of the great things about travel is that it allows the traveler to meet new people, and in doing so, learn to see the world differently. Working at the computer all day, sometimes my only contact with another human being is when the pizza is delivered. I hadn't realized it, but I had begun to lose my faith in humanity. My travels with Cynthia gave me an opportunity to meet people and to regain a more balanced view of the world.

A perfect example of this happened while riding on the Lagrange Rail-Trail near Medford, Maine. After a long and difficult ride, we came across a beautiful trestle bridge that afforded us a breathtaking view of the river gorge and surrounding countryside. It was one of those moments that make a trip like this worth the effort. After soaking in the natural beauty, we crossed the bridge. When we got to the other side there was a woman parked in her Jeep. She apparently had been waiting for us to cross the bridge. We stopped to thank her for waiting, and we told her how nice it was for her to wait. She looked at us briefly and decided that we were not from the area. She spoke in a slow, clear, and reassuring voice. She said, "Being nice is a way of life in Maine."

The woman in the Jeep was right. People are nice in Maine. During the trip, we met so many other wonderful people on and off the trails. They helped me to regain a more balanced view of the world. At the end of the trip, as I was unpacking my suitcase, I found my cell phone and saw that the batteries were dead. I had been too busy enjoying my trip and recharging my personal batteries to remember to recharge the cell phone's batteries. Now that's a vacation.

10 Woodabogan Rail-Trail

This forested trail parallels the Carrabassett River. A favorite trail for cross-country skiers in the winter, in warmer months the path is enjoyed by mountain bikers and hikers. (Skiers need to purchase a trail-use permit at Sugarloaf prior to using the trail. Call 207–237–6830 for information.)

Activities:

Location: Franklin County

Length: 7 miles

Surface: Original ballast and gravel

Wheelchair access: No

Difficulty: Moderate

Food: None

Rest rooms: At the playground near the Carrabassett Valley Town Office and at Sugarloaf's Ski Touring Center.

Seasons: Open year-round.

Access and parking: From Farmington take State Route 4/27 north. Where Route 4 and 27 diverge, turn right to stay on Route 27 and go approximately 30 miles to Kingfield. Go through Kingfield and continue another 5 miles to Carrabassett Valley. The Carrabassett River is on your right. In another 4 miles, look for a small sign for the Carrabassett Valley Town Office. Turn right. Parking is available at the Town Office, where you will also find picnic tables and a playground.

Rentals: Cross-country skis and snowshoes can be rented at Sugarloaf's Ski Touring Center; (207) 237–2000.

Contact: Carrabassett River Trail (Woodabogan Rail-Trail) Outdoor Center, Sugarloaf/USA Touring Center, RR 1, Box 5000, Kingfield, ME 04947-9799; (207) 237–6830; e-mail: outdoor@somtel.com.

• •

The Woodabogan Trail is part of a 50-mile network of cross-country trails managed by the Sugarloaf/USA Ski Touring Center. The trail offers a pleasant respite for nature seekers wanting to spend time in a beautiful part of the Maine countryside.

TOBOGGAN TRAIL

If you think *Woodabogan* is an unusual name for a rail-trail, you're right. Formerly called the Carrabassett River Trail, and commonly referred to as the Narrow Gauge Trail, the Woodabogan Trail acquired its latest—and official—name as a tribute to the Penobscot Indians who once inhabited this part of Maine. The name translates to "toboggan trail," and it is one of dozens of trails with Penobscot names run by the Sugarloaf/USA Touring Center. If you venture onto the 50-mile cross-country ski trail network, you will encounter trails with names like Gwipdez ("colored leaf"), Damakguay ("beaver"), Wezinauks ("go fast"), and one that you may want to avoid: Jezhawuk, which means "mosquito."

The trail is built on one of the Sandy River/Rangeley Lakes Railroad's many narrow-gauge routes that originated in Farmington. The railroad company served two primary industries: logging and tourism. It hauled timber and other goods to Farmington, where they were transferred to standard railroads for transport to other destinations in the Northeast. The narrow-gauge line also ferried passengers to the many resort hotels in the Rangeley district. Both industries were already faltering when the Great Depression began, and the Sandy River/Rangeley Lakes Railroad went out of business in the mid-1930s. While the corridor was used informally as a trail for many years, it was not until 1983 that efforts were made to improve the corridor and maintain it for recreational use.

To get to the trail, turn left onto the road from the parking lot and make another left onto Huston Brook Road. After you pass several small chalets, the Carrabassett River appears on the left. Continue on the road, which now doubles as a trail, for about 1 mile. Turn left when the road forks. This is the official beginning of the Woodabogan Trail.

After crossing a creek, the trail winds uphill and away from the river through a forest of oak, beech, maple, white pine, aspen, and birch. These trees display a stunning array of color during the early fall. Within a half-mile the river comes back into view on the left.

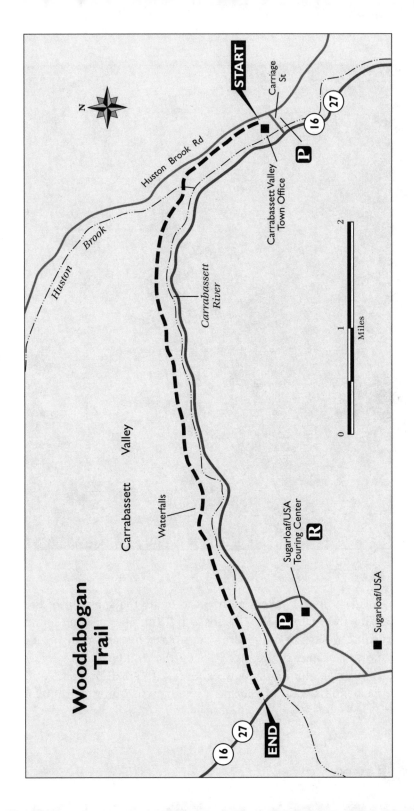

The Woodabogan Trail can be enjoyed by families.

Just past mile 2, take a moment to enjoy the splendor of the cascading waterfalls on the Carrabassett River. The soothing sound of rushing water not only calms the senses, but also drowns out any noise from nearby Route 27. Soon the trail becomes narrow and the surface temporarily overflows with small boulders and stumps before smoothing out near another cascading swirl at 2.4 miles.

At the 3-mile mark, a steep rocky wall lines the right side of the trail. The trail begins to level out within another half-mile, although the surface continues to alternate between moderately smooth and quite rocky. At 4.5 miles, the trail veers away from the river to cut through a wooded wetland. Take a moment to try to spot a pileated woodpecker and other birds. A moose or a deer may also make an appearance if you're lucky.

At the 4.5-mile mark, consider taking a detour to the Sugarloaf/USA Touring Center. The center has a number of additional trails to explore. In addition, the views from the center's lodge are spectacular—including such peaks as Moose Bog, Sugarloaf Mountain, Brunt Mountain, and Crocker Mountain.

You'll need to pay close attention to the signs to get to the touring center. From the original trail, look for a sign for Trail 25 (Intersection B–E) on the left. Follow this trail through a residential area, and after crossing Route 27 (Intersection A–Z), continue on the trail as it crosses Trail 7 (Intersection A–X). Go straight until you reach Intersection F, then bear right until the path merges with Trail 5 about 100 yards before the lodge.

Back on the trail, just before the 6-mile mark, the trail passes an area marked by extensive beaver activity. The trail, which is still on an incline, is wet in this area, with some water holes and an occasional log in the corridor. In another half-mile you will reach a gate that will lead to the Bigelow Train Station (adjacent to Route 27). The main entrance to the Sugarloaf/USA ski resort is to the left. The trail appears to continue on the other side of Route 27, but this is actually an access road for the Sugarloaf Golf Course.

If you turn right onto Route 27, you can reach the Appalachian Trail in 2 miles. This famous back-country hiking trail continues all the way to Georgia. If you are turning around and retracing your steps, have fun—but be careful—as the trail drops steadily downhill almost all the way back.

MORE RAIL-TRAILS

F Aroostook Valley Trail and Bangor/ Aroostook Trail

This trail is wonderfully isolated. If you want to be far away from the maddening crowd, this is the place.

Activities:

Location: Aroostook County

Length: 71.5 miles (loop)

Surface: Varies, but primarily dirt

Wheelchair access: None

Difficulty: Easy but long

Food: Restaurants and food stores are available in the towns of Caribou, Woodland, New Sweden, Washburn, Perham, Stockholm, and Van Buren.

Rest rooms: Some rest rooms can be found in restaurants or gas stations in the towns of Caribou, Woodland, New Sweden, Washburn, Perham, Stockholm, and Van Buren.

Seasons: Open year-round.

Access and parking: Take I–95 north to exit 58, Route 11. Follow Route 11 north and turn right onto Route 227 east. Continue on 227 east to the intersection with Route 164 north and turn left. Parking is available along Route 164 in Washburn, where a trailhead marks the beginning of the trail.

Rentals: Ski Shop, 31 Main Street, Van Buren, ME; (207) 868–2737.

Transportation: Cyr Bus Line provides service between Bangor and Caribou; (207) 827–2335 or (800) 259–8687; cyrbus@telplus.net.

Contact: Caribou Parks and Recreation Department; (207) 493–4225.

The trail follows the route of the county's only electric railroad through wooded areas and open fields. The Aroostook Valley Railroad built this portion of the line in 1910. Converting to diesel operation in 1946, it later discontinued passenger service and was abandoned in 1982.

The definitive word here is remote. The Aroostook Valley Trail is located in the northernmost part of Maine. It is 71.5 miles long and connects the towns of Caribou, Woodland, New Sweden, Washburn, Perham, Stockholm, and Van Buren. The trail's scenery traverses farmlands, crosses streams, and passes through a variety of woodland and wetland habitats. The Nature Conservancy Woodland Bog Preserve is a favorite site for bird watchers. More than eighty species of birds are known to make their homes there. Following the trail past Salmon Brook and the Salmon Brook Bog, travelers will enjoy a riotous diversity of native flora and fauna. The Madawaska River follows the trail from Blackstone Siding to Stockholm, offering panoramic vistas. Watch for moose, muskrats, and beavers. A favorite trail among cyclists during the warmer months, it's also enjoyed by ATV enthusiasts year-round, but especially during the winter. Be sure to carry a good supply of insect repellent during the late spring and summer—blackflies and mosquitoes are abundant. Cyclists should carry spare parts and a repair kit, and should watch out for the occasional ATV.

Ⓖ Calais Waterfront Walkway

A short but picture-perfect rail-trail from start to finish.

Activities:

Location: Washington County

Length: 1.5 miles

Surface: Asphalt

Wheelchair access: Yes, but the surface is best in the first mile.

Difficulty: Easy

Food: Restaurants and food stores are available in Calais.

Rest rooms: Rest rooms are located at the Tourist Information Bureau at the start of the trail.

Seasons: Open year-round.

Access and parking: Follow Route 1 into downtown Calais. At the intersection of Route 1 and Union Street, turn onto Union Street. Turn into the parking lot for the Maine Publicity Bureau at 7 Union Street. The lot is behind the building. To the left of the parking lot is a sign that says THE CALAIS WATERFRONT WALKWAY. Take a left to begin the trail.

Rentals: None

Contact: Call Louis Bernardini at (207) 454–2844 or Jim Porter at (207) 454–2521.

• • • • • • • • • • • • • • • • • • • •

Once a busy lumbering port, Calais (the name of the town is pronounced kal-iss) saw its first railway—the Calais and Baring Railroad—built in 1839. In the 1890s, Calais was connected to Bangor via the Washington County Railroad, which was later purchased by the Maine Central Railroad. The line was abandoned in the 1970s.

This short, sweet 1.5-mile-long rail-trail is a jewel in Calais' crown. It's a pretty trail, passing along the St. Croix River. It goes through the Main Street Underpass—take note of the stonework here, which dates from the late nineteenth century. There's a wonderful diversity of flora and fauna along the trail. Be especially on the lookout for bald eagles scanning the water for prey. The trail is wheelchair-accessible, with tie edging and a hard-packed, crushed-stone surface over the first mile. Current plans call for the expansion of the Calais Waterfront Walkway with an additional 3 miles of trail.

Ⓗ Old Narrow Gauge Volunteer Trail

This trail needs some tender loving care. The town of Randolph is planning to fix up and expand the trail.

Activities:

Location: Kennebec County

Length: 1.25 miles

Surface: Dirt, with parts overgrown by grass

Wheelchair access: No

Difficulty: Moderate. As the trail is somewhat overgrown, it takes some time to walk through areas of the path that may be muddy. In dryer weather, look out for potholes along the trail.

Food: There are several small restaurants and convenience stores in Randolph.

Rest rooms: None

Seasons: Open year-round.

Access and parking: From I–95, take Route 128 for 3 miles until you reach Route 226. Turn left onto Route 226 and continue to the town of Randolph. Go about 0.5 mile until you see a dip in the road at Windsor Street Crossing. The trail begins at this point.

Rentals: None

Contact: Town of Randolph; (207) 582–5808.

• •

This 1.25-mile trail in Randolph was established in 1985 as a nature trail and follows the route of the old Kennebec Central Railroad line. The narrow-gauge Kennebec Central began service in 1890 and served the dual purpose of hauling coal and taking visitors to the National Soldiers Home in Togus. When the government gave the coal delivery contract to a trucking company in 1929, the railroad couldn't maintain its business and the line was abandoned. The tracks were removed in 1933. While the trail is short and in need of maintenance, the residents of the small town of Randolph are excited about it. Don't be surprised if the trail is upgraded and expanded in the future.

Future Maine Rail-Trails

There are plenty of projects in the works in Maine.

The Westbrook to Fryeburg trail is in its initial planning stages. The trail would follow Route 202 in Windham to the Maine/New Hampshire border in Fryeburg.

Fort Kent, in the northernmost section of the state, is planning to develop 18 miles of rail-trail.

A 47.1-mile trail from Kittery to South Portland is also being planned. This trail will be part of the East Coast Greenway, and will utilize the roadbed of the long-abandoned Eastern Railroad.

Look forward to the Brewer to Calais Rail-Trail, which has been receiving considerable media attention. The 125-mile trail would provide access to Tunk Lake, Donnell Pond, and Schoodic Mountain.

The Kennebec River Rail-Trail between Gardner and Augusta is in the planning stage. The Lewiston-Auburn area has several projects brewing, including the Lewiston-Lisbon Rail-Trail. A Lewiston-Auburn Rail-Trail would include a nine-acre park that would connect with a bicycle-pedestrian trail. The nearby town of Norway is also planning a rail-trail project.

Other proposals include a rail-trail in the town of Pittsfield and a rail-trail following the old rail bed between Camden and Rockport on Penobscot Bay.

Rails-to-Trails

MASSACHUSETTS

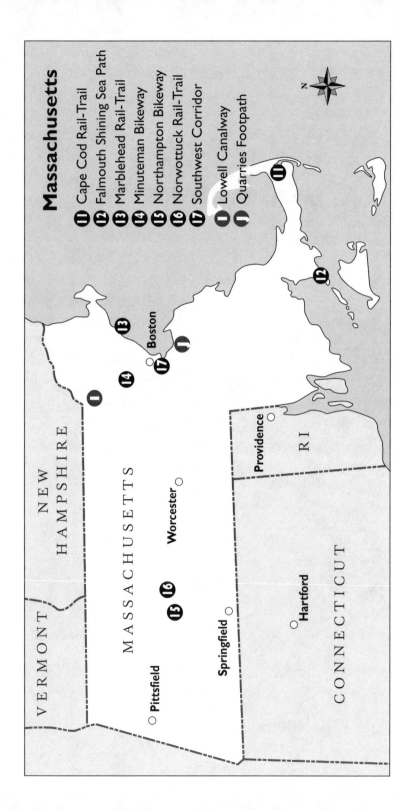

INTRODUCTION

Massachusetts is a glorious state, full of forests, lakes, and ponds, and boasting a coastline of famous beauty. The people of Massachusetts are proud of their state and much effort has been made to preserve and enhance its many charms.

Traveling to the southeast portion of the state and visiting Cape Cod, Martha's Vineyard, or Nantucket is a feast for the senses. Waves crash along the coast, and sailboats and fishing boats dot the horizon. Equally beautiful is the northern coast, with such picturesque towns as Marblehead and Rockport.

Boston is a wonderful city full of history and cultural attractions. The Freedom Trail in downtown Boston will take you past many of the city's historic sites. Just north of Boston is Lexington and Concord, where the first battle of the American Revolution was fought. Rolling hills, ponds and lakes, farmland, and elegant homes define the area. Walden Pond was Henry David Thoreau's famous retreat. Louisa May Alcott wrote *Little Women* from her home in Concord. To the west are the Berkshires, Massachusetts's only mountainous area, famous for its rural charm.

Massachusetts rail-trails are user friendly. In October 1998 there were twelve rail-trails open to the public, nearly 120 miles of trails in all. In the Cape Cod region are the well-established Falmouth Shining Sea Trail between Woods Hole and Falmouth, and the Cape Cod Rail-Trail, which runs from Dennis to Wellfleet. Both trails offer plenty of opportunities to explore diversity of the Cape Cod region.

In Boston, the urban Southwest Corridor is a testament to the strong advocacy of environmental groups who sought to bring a rail-trail to the city. Nearby, between Arlington and Bedford, is the Minuteman Rail-Trail.

Farther west, the Norwottuck and Northampton rail-trails traverse the central part of the state, offering the traveler a sample of the rural side of Massachusetts.

More rail-trails are being developed in Massachusetts, with a projected additional sixty trails covering 496 miles.

Massachusetts's

· · · · · · · · · · · · · · · · ·

TOP RAIL-TRAILS

11 Cape Cod Rail-Trail

Among the most scenic recreation trails in Massachusetts and a favorite with cyclists and day hikers, the Cape Cod Trail provides access to beaches, fresh water ponds, cranberry bogs and wild wetlands, quiet villages, and some of the best bird watching in the state. Anglers may want to try their luck on North Pond, where bass and panfish can be caught from shore.

Activities:

Location: Barnstable and Howard Counties

Length: 26 miles from the western end at East Harwich to the eastern end of the rail-trail at Wellfleet

Surface: Asphalt

Wheelchair access: Yes

Difficulty: Easy

Food: A variety of restaurant and small groceries are available close to the trail in Harwich, Brewster, Orleans, and Wellfleet. Street vendors in Harwich sell everything from hot dogs to lobster rolls during the summer. Some restaurants are closed from October to April.

Rest rooms: Wheelchair-accessible public rest rooms with running water are located at Nickerson State Park and just off the trail in Harwich, Brewster, Orleans, Eastham, and Wellfleet. Portable chemical toilets are maintained at the trailhead in Wellfleet during the summer months.

Seasons: Open year-round. The trail will probably be snow-packed and icy from December through March. It is used most during the summer months; however, local residents often prefer autumn on the trail when

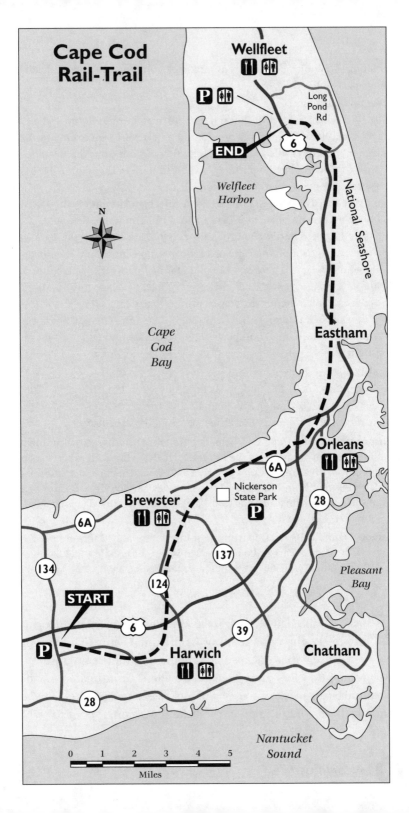

fall colors and cooler daytime temperatures combine to make a special outdoor experience.

Access and parking:

- *East Harwich access:* From Route 6 east, turn right onto Route 134 and travel 0.4 mile to the parking area on the left. Overflow parking in the summer months is allowed in the long turnout opposite the entrance to the parking lot, but no parking is allowed here in the winter. This is the western end of the Cape Cod Rail-Trail.
- *Nickerson State Park access:* From Route 6 east, turn left onto Route 124 at Harwich and go 4.1 miles to Brewster. Turn right on Route 6A and go 2.4 miles to the gated entrance of Nickerson State Park on the right. Park in the first parking lot on the right or in the overflow lot behind the ranger building on the left. There is a $2.00 fee for day parking. The state park opens at 7:00 A.M. year-round and closes at 6:00 P.M. except from May 1 to September 30, when it stays open until 9:00 P.M.
- *Wellfleet access:* Take Route 6 east through Eastham. The parking lot is 0.2 mile past the Long Pond boat ramp, which is marked by a sign on the right.

Rentals:

- Rail-Trail Bike Shop, 302 Underpass Road, Brewster, MA; (508) 896–8200.
- Little Capistrano Bike Shop, Salt Pond Road, Eastham, MA; (508) 255–6515.
- Orleans Cycle, 26 Main Street, Orleans, MA; (508) 255–9115.

Transportation: The Cape Cod Regional Transit Authority provides transportation to nearby portions of the rail-trail. The H2O Line offers service on Route 28, from Hyannis to Orleans. Call (800) 352–7155 for more information. The Plymouth and Brockton Line provides service from Boston and Hyannis to outlying areas of Cape Cod. An extra $5.00 per bicycle is charged. Call (508) 771–6191 for details.

Contact: Danny O'Brien, Department of Environmental Management, Division of Forests and Parks, 100 Cambridge Street, Boston, MA 02202; (617) 727–3180 or (800) 831–0569; www.magnet.state.ma.us/dem.htm.

· ·

The Cape Cod Rail-Trail offers its travelers the perfect opportunity to see the Cape in all of its pristine beauty. The best of the Cape Cod region is encapsulated here—and there's no traffic!

The Cape Cod Rail-Trail gives its travelers an intimate view of the natural beauty of the Cape. As the trail passes salt marshes, ponds, cranberry bogs, and ultimately the Atlantic Ocean, the visitor will see some of the very best that the area has to offer.

The trail follows the route of the former Old Colony Railroad, which carried passengers from Boston to Wellfleet in 1870 and all the way to Provincetown three years later. The train service opened up the area to travelers and brought droves of tourists from Boston. Passenger service ended in 1937 as tourists began to bring their automobiles to the Cape. Railroad freight service continued for another twenty-five years before the line was discontinued. The Massachusetts Department of Environmental Management revitalized the route as a trail and it is now a very popular route for people of all ages.

The trail begins in East Harwich among pines, maples, and oaks. The two stone whistle posts, each with an etched "W," once signaled train engineers to blow their whistles. Just beyond the half-mile mark, the trail crosses two busy roads, so use caution. The pleasant scent of pine quickly returns after you cross the Herring River. At 1.5 miles, the trail passes Sand Pond. Birds are plentiful and a mix of wetland vegetation surrounds the trail before making way for a cranberry bog just before the 2.5-mile mark. Within a mile the trail passes through a corrugated metal tunnel.

A 100-year-old cranberry bog is situated to the right of the trail just past 5.5 miles. It gets its water from Hinckley's Pond, which features a sandy beach on the trail's left side. It's a perfect place to take a break. Or continue another mile to the Pleasant Lake General Store, which offers soft drinks, a deli, ice cream, and snacks. The store has been a popular stop since the railroad era.

The 716-acre Long Pond, the second-largest freshwater lake on Cape Cod, borders the right side of the trail corridor while Seymour Pond and a welcoming public beach soon appear on the left. The trail now parallels Brewster Center. This charming town offers a quintessential Cape Cod experience. A general store in the town's center has turn-of-the century charm, with many gift items and some very tasty fudge. Several eateries are available on Route 6A. To get to Brewster, take a left when the trail intersects Route 137. There is a parking lot at the intersection of Long Pond Road and Underpass Road.

Nickerson Park is located at 11 miles and warrants a stop. The park boasts lakes, public beaches, and campsites. For people planning to camp here, a reservation is necessary as the campsites fill up months in advance. Call (508) 896–3491 for more information.

The next 2 miles are among the trail's most scenic. Much of the land is protected by the State Park. Red maples and black gum trees dot the swampy land, which is a haven for warblers, thrushes, and red-winged blackbirds. Namskaket Creek creates the border between Brewster and Orleans.

The trail takes a short detour while crossing U.S. Route 6 before proceeding to Main Street in Orleans. The center of town offers a number of shops and restaurants. To continue toward Eastham, turn left onto Main Street—use caution on this heavily-traveled road. The road leads to Rock Harbor and Skaget Beach, located at the 14-mile mark.

The trail resumes, following power lines for about a mile. Because of this, much of the trailside vegetation has been cleared, making this section of trail very sunny and hot in the summer. This area is surrounded by salt marshes. Sand dunes can be seen in the dis-

Long Pond is one of several inland lakes lining the Cape Cod Rail-Trail.

tance on the trail's right side. Beyond mile 18, the trail is flanked by Great Pond on the left and Long Pond on the right.

The trail then passes the Coast Guard Beach, part of the Cape Cod National Seashore. A visitor center is located about 0.25 mile down the road and the seashore is about 3 miles away.

The Cape Cod Trail continues about 6 miles north toward Wellfleet. This section is visually less interesting than the rest, in part because power lines parallel this section and the vegetation is sparse. The northern end, however, does offer additional opportunities to get to the National Seashore. It also offers an alternative for people wishing to avoid Route 6 from Wellfleet to Orleans, a road that can be extremely congested during the summer months.

The trail ends in less than 2 miles at a large parking lot. To the left is a fruit stand, general store, and a post office with pay phones.

Not surprisingly, there are several interesting side trips you might consider to conclude your Cape Cod Rail-Trail experience. Follow the sign to the right of the parking lot leading to "Beaches." In about a mile, you will arrive at the Cape Cod Seashore. The beach can be your tour's final destination; the Atlantic shore is quite beautiful and worth a vacation visit. There are also several off-the-beaten path inland lakes where swimming is encouraged.

Enjoy the brilliant views of the Nantucket and Vineyard Sounds on this short trail connecting Falmouth and Woods Hole.

Activities:

Location: Barnstable County

Length: 4 miles

Surface: Asphalt

Wheelchair access: Yes

Difficulty: Easy

Food: An assortment of restaurants, coffeehouses, taverns, and take-out establishments are available in both Falmouth and Woods Hole.

Rest rooms: Steamship Ferry Dock, Woods Hole

Seasons: Open year-round.

Access and parking: The best place to park is at the ferry shuttle Palmer Parking lot in Falmouth (on Route 28). An additional trail parking lot is available on Locust Street, just past downtown Falmouth.

Rentals:

- Falmouth Shining Sea Corner Cycle, 115 Palmer Avenue, Falmouth, MA; (508) 540–4195.
- Holiday Cycle, 465 Grand Avenue, Falmouth, MA; (508) 540–3549.

Transportation: The Bonanza Bus offers service from Boston, New York, and Providence. While luggage gets first priority, bicycles can be transported by the bus for an additional $3.00. Call (800) 556–3815 for more information.

Contact: Kevin Lynch, Chairman, Falmouth Bikeway Committee, Town Hall, Falmouth, MA 02540; (508) 968–5293.

• •

This short trail is exceptionally pretty, with wonderful views of the Nantucket and Vineyard Sounds. It is a perfect way to travel from Woods Hole and Falmouth during the summer months when traffic is snarled and everyone is clamoring to get to the Woods Hole Ferry Terminal.

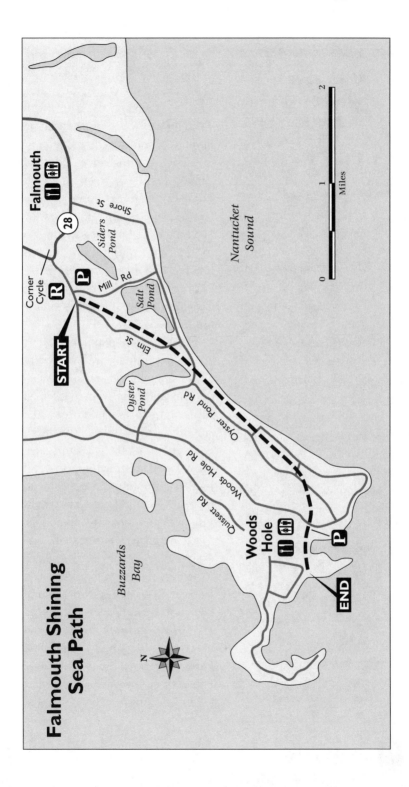

UP AND DOWN ISLAND ON MARTHA'S VINEYARD

Martha's Vineyard is just a forty-five minute ferry ride away and is a wonderful resort community. Vineyard Haven, Oak Bluffs, and Edgartown are considered the "down island" towns. Vineyard Haven has a pleasant Main Street and plenty of restaurants and shops. Oak Bluffs is funky and fun. Be sure to visit the Campground, a special treat with its gingerbread cottages. Edgartown is the jewel in the crown, a beautiful town full of historic homes, churches, and museums. Edgartown was a favorite town among Massachusetts sea captains, whose homes still adorn its residential streets.

"Up Island" comprises the communities of West Tisbury, Chilmark, Menemsha, and Aquinnah (formerly known as Gay Head). This part of the Vineyard is more rural. Picture long stretches of farm land, stone walls alongside the roads, and trees everywhere. There are plenty of seascapes too.

The corridor was built more than a century ago in 1884 as an extension of the Old Colony Line. The train served the area from 1872 until 1959. A group of wealthy families banded together to request exclusive train service. The Old Colony Railroad agreed and what quickly became known as the "Dude Train" originated. The New Haven Railroad purchased the line in 1892 and maintained the exclusive services for such distinguished people as President Grover Cleveland and members of his Cabinet.

As the Cape's popularity grew, additional trains were eventually added, although none were as elaborate as the Dude Train. It stopped running in 1916, while other passenger service trains continued through the 1950s. The trains also provided local transportation and hauled shipments of ice, coal, and farm-raised and sea-harvested products to major off-Cape cities. These freight cars persisted for several more years. The track and ties were eventually removed in 1972, nearly 100 years after the rail line began. The trail was dedicated in 1975 as a community project. The bikeway was named in honor of Falmouth born Katherine Lee Bates who wrote the poem "America the Beautiful." The poem was later set to music. Borrowing from the lyrics "from sea to shining sea," the trail was aptly named.

The trail begins in a wooded setting with an occasional Cape Cod home. The trail crosses Locust Street (also known as Woods Holes Road Crossing), where additional parking is available. Shortly thereafter, the trail passes the Modes Hatch House. This home is thought to be the oldest in the area, and was built around 1690. The land was originally bought from the Indians and settled in 1660. It was incorporated under the name Suckanesset meaning "where the black wampum is found." Soon the trail reaches Salt Pond, which was actually a depression formed in the Ice Age. Swans and otters nest along and glide upon Salt Pond, which was once a sea inlet.

After the at-grade crossing at Elm Street, the Vineyard Sound will come into view, absolutely one of the prettiest sights in all of New England. Another smaller body of water but equally alluring is Oyster Pond, making its appearance on the right. This pond is also home to various water fowl such as white and yellow perch, herring sunfish and eels. Nearby marshes host frogs and turtles. Benches have been placed along this section of the trail.

Leaving Woods Hole.

After crossing Surf Drive, the trail closely aligns itself with the ocean. Take some time to breathe the salty air or take a quick dip in the ocean. The trail parallels the beach for a little more than a half-mile before veering back inland.

Soon, young pine oaks and sugar maples line the route again as it meanders inland. The trail joins a parking lot reserved for Vineyard-bound travelers before opening onto the Woods Hole Harbor. Hop the ferry to Martha's Vineyard, a bike-friendly island and a perfect place for day trippers.

Take time to enjoy the views along the Falmouth Shining Sea Path.

Marblehead is one of the nicest beach communities north of Boston. This trail forks in two directions. Both branches are pretty, and both eventually lead to the Atlantic Ocean.

Activities:

Location: Essex County

Length: 5 miles from Marblehead to the Swampscott fork; 3 miles from Marblehead to Salem

Surface: Packed gravel

Wheelchair access: While it may be difficult at times to navigate the wheelchair through the gravel, with tenacity a wheelchair user could enjoy the path.

Difficulty: Easy

Food: An assortment of restaurants and fast-food stores are available just prior to the trail's starting point. An additional store and restaurant can be reached at the Smith Street crossing, about 1.6 miles from the beginning of the trail.

Rest rooms: None

Seasons: Open year-round.

Access and parking: Head north on Route 1A to the intersection of Paradise Road and Vinnin Street. Turn right on Vinnin Street. Continue on Vinnin until it turns into Pleasant Street. At Bessom Street, turn left and go past a shopping plaza. Parking is available adjacent to the shopping center.

Rentals: Marblehead Cycle, 25 Bessom Street, Marblehead, MA; (781) 631–1570.

Contact: Marblehead Rail-Trail (The Path), Tom Hammond, Superintendent of Recreation, Marblehead Department of Recreation, Park and Forest, 10 Humphrey Street, Marblehead, MA 01945-1906; (781) 631–3350; fax (781) 639–3420.

• • • • • • • • • • • • • • • • • • • •

The charm of this trail is its sense of suburban peace. As you follow the path, you can hear children playing in the backyards and neighbors chatting over their fences. The path is used by many of the local families. Mothers with strollers are among the most frequent users of the path.

The Eastern Rail Road built this line as the Swampscott Branch in 1873. However, the Eastern Rail Road was facing bankruptcy and the line was bought by the B&M branch in 1884. Passenger service remained intact until 1959, but was abandoned in 1961.

The trail begins just south of the parking lot on the other side of Bessom Street. About 100 feet after crossing the street, the trail passes under the Village Street overpass. The fork in the path is just past the overpass. Take the path to the left to head toward the Marblehead Beach at the Marblehead/Swampscott border.

Initially, the trail passes through a residential area with houses on both sides of the trail. At 1.1 miles, use caution while crossing Route 114 at Pleasant Street. This is one of the main thoroughfares in the area, and the automobiles pass swiftly. There is a crosswalk to help trail users get across the street.

At 1.6 miles, the trail crosses Smith Street. The Marblehead Post Office is here, as is a convenience store and a small restaurant.

Take a moment at the 2-mile mark to look at the original granite post on the right, the only indication on the trail that a railroad once passed through here.

The Marblehead Community Center on the right, at 2.3 miles, offers sport opportunities for the neighborhood youth. The wide-open field is mainly used for soccer games.

The trail again widens as it passes homes on both sides of the trail. Since there are fewer trees in this area, wear a hat for shade in the summer months.

For the next mile the path becomes more shaded, with trees and plants on both sides. At 3.6 miles, the path stops for a short period, at the Emanuel Temple parking lot. Follow the one-way street past the temple. The trail resumes at 4.0 miles at a marked crosswalk. The path borders homes again for the next half-mile, with a small ravine on the right. At 4.6 miles, the trail ends. Take a left onto Seaview Street for 0.4 mile to reach the Marblehead Beach. A small park is situated on a bluff overlooking the sea. This is a perfect place to rest before returning. Or bring a swimsuit and take a refreshing dip in the ocean at the beach just below the park.

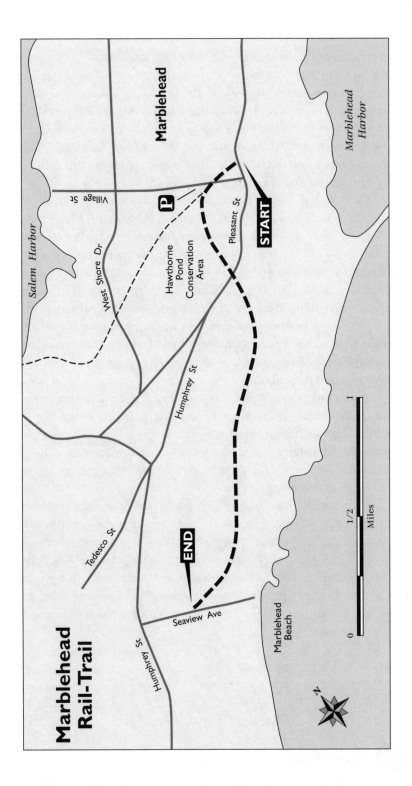

Marblehead
Rail-Trail

Marblehead

Salem Harbor

Village St

West Shore Dr

P

Hawthorne
Pond
Conservation
Area

Pleasant St

START

Humphrey St

Marblehead
Harbor

Tedesco St

END

Humphrey St

Seaview Ave

Marblehead
Beach

N

0   1/2   1

Miles

For travelers interested in taking the fork toward Salem, the path is shorter and is only 2 miles. At the fork in the trail after the Village Street overpass, take a right. For the first mile you will pass through the Hawthorne Pond Conservation area on the left. It is pretty here.

At 1 mile, you will cross Route 114. Be very careful crossing the highway; cars travel quickly. The trail borders a residential area on the right. To the left is Gatchell Park, where Little League softball games are often played. The trail becomes particularly scenic at the end of the trail, where the Forest River and the Salem Harbor meet. You'll cross over two short bridges before reaching the trail's end. The first bridge has an interesting history: A local farmer wanted his cattle to graze at the water's edge. The train, however, passed through his property, meaning the cattle could only get to the other side by crossing over active railroad tracks. Thus, the bridge was constructed, and the cattle would go under the bridge to reach the harbor. The cattle and the farm are long gone. In recent years, the bridge was rebuilt by the Marblehead Municipal Light Company in conjunction with the development of the rail-trail.

The trail ends at the intersection of Route 114 and Rosedale Avenue, at the border of Marblehead and Salem. If you would like to combine the two forks into one trip, you might want to consider beginning your trip here. After traveling the first 2 miles, take a sharp left just before the Village Street overpass and make your way to the Swampscott border.

An additional 2-mile trail, which is not part of the rail-trail network but is equally fun and scenic, is the bike path that passes through the Marblehead Neck area. The path will take you past an Audubon Sanctuary and near a park at the Marblehead Light House. From the Bessom Street parking lot in Marblehead, take a left onto Bessom Street and then a right onto Pleasant Street. Travel a short distance until you see Ocean Avenue on your left. The bike path begins just past Devereux Beach.

A TRAVELER'S "MUST SEES"

The towns of Marblehead and Salem are "must see" destinations on a vacationing traveler's itinerary. Both are rich in history and charm.

Marblehead, a popular yachting and vacation town, was an early center of American seagoing commerce. Its name comes from the marblelike cliffs of the town's distinctive headland. Founded in 1629 by settlers from the English Channel Islands, Marblehead was by 1660 perhaps the key fishing town in New England. Hundreds of splendid homes dating from the eighteenth and early nineteenth centuries still bear witness to the town's prosperity. During the American Revolution, the Marblehead seamen distinguished themselves by their service in the Continental Army. The amphibious Marbleheaders played a crucial role in saving the army during the evacuation of Long Island, and later shuttled the army safely back and forth across the icy Delaware River to attack the Hessian and British troops at Trenton and Princeton. Today, Marblehead's charming downtown district offers the traveler a wide choice of restaurants, boutiques, and gift shops.

Salem is perhaps best known for the infamous 1692 witchcraft trials. The Salem Witch Museum, located at Washington Square, gives the visitor a thrilling—and troubling—look at the witchcraft hysteria that resulted in the execution of twenty people. Call (978) 744–1692 for more information. Also of interest is the House of Seven Gables, the home of Nathaniel Hawthorne. Tours are available. Call (978) 744–0991. Salem also boasts fine restaurants, a museum and landmarks highlighting the town's seafaring tradition, and a very popular Halloween celebration.

14 Minuteman Bikeway

The Minuteman Bikeway has it all. It's close to Boston, it's historic, it's located in a lush and beautiful area, and it's great for families. Its historical significance is of particular note. The trail closely approximates the route Paul Revere took on his famous ride in 1775, announcing the incursion by British forces and heralding the beginning of the American Revolution.

Activities:

Location: Middlesex County

Length: 11 miles

Surface: Asphalt

Wheelchair access: Yes

Difficulty: Easy

Food: A variety of restaurants, ice cream shops, and eateries are available close to the trail in Arlington, Lexington, and Bedford.

Rest rooms: The Visitor Center in Lexington Center and at the Alewife Station in Arlington.

Seasons: Open year-round. The trail may be more difficult to traverse during the winter months. It is used most heavily during the summer and autumn months. It is particularly pretty during the fall, when the foliage bursts into color.

Access and parking:

- *Alewife Transit access:* The Alewife Transit Station (known as the "T") offers affordable parking and is about 1.5 miles from downtown Arlington. The T station is located at the intersection of the Concord Turnpike and Route 16.
- *Arlington access:* From the west, take Route 60 north from Route 2 (the Concord Turnpike). Travel 1 mile to Massachusetts Avenue. A municipal lot is located just past Massachusetts Avenue on the right side, behind the Arlington Visitor Center. From the east, exit I–93 at Route 60 west. Follow Route 60 for 4 miles. The municipal parking lot is just before Massachusetts Avenue, on the left.

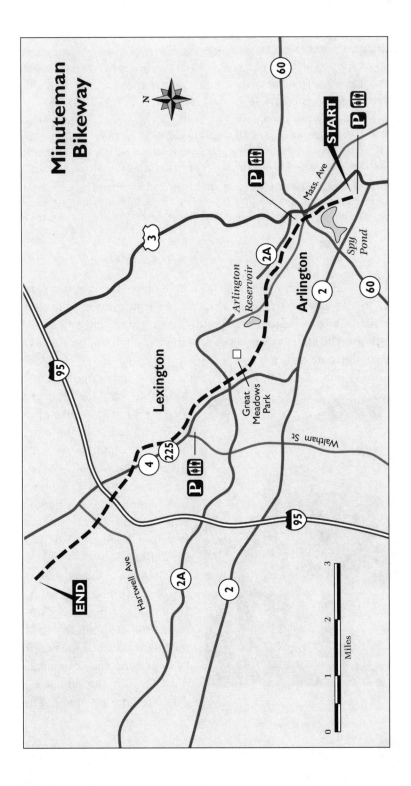

Rentals:

- Bikeway Cycle and Sports, 3 Bow Street, Lexington, MA; (781) 861–1199.
- The Bike Stops Here, 43 Dudley Street, Arlington, MA; (781) 643–4328.
- The Bikeway Source, 111 South Road, Bedford, MA; (781) 275–7799.

Transportation: The MBTA's Red Line will take you to the beginning of the trail at Alewife Station. You can bring a bike on the T by showing a Bike Pass ($5.00 buys a pass for four years). Bike passes are available at the Special Pass Office (617–722–5438) at the Downtown Crossing station on weekdays.

Contact: Daniel O'Brien, Bikeway and Rail-Trail Planner, Department of Environmental Management, Division of Resource Conservation, 100 Cambridge Street, Room 1404, Boston, MA 02202-0044; (617) 727–1388; fax (617) 727–2630.

• •

The Minuteman Bikeway is located in one of the prettiest parts of Massachusetts. Only a couple miles northwest of Boston, the bikeway runs past several ponds, lakes, parks, and wildflower meadows. The bikeway begins in Arlington, a suburb of Boston, and ends in the more rural town of Bedford. Crossing Route 128, the Massachusetts hub of technological business, the current and past history of the state blends.

Lexington Station.

The Minuteman Bikeway—named in honor of the patriots who fought in the American Revolution—took its own place in history when it was named America's 500th Rail-Trail during the National Rail-Trail Celebration in October 1992.

The West Lexington and Arlington Railroad opened in 1846, connecting West Cambridge to Lexington. By 1874, the line was extend to Bedford by the Boston and Lowell Railroad. The line carried passengers, freight, and mail. The

Wildflowers flourish throughout much of the Great Meadows.

Boston & Maine Railroad provided service from 1887 until 1958. A storm in 1977 shut down passenger service, and the line was virtually closed thereafter. Then, after years of delay, the Minuteman Bikeway opened in 1992 amid great fanfare.

The trail begins just north of the Alewife T Station. After crossing Lake Street, notice the stone curbing along the trail's edge. This once marked the perimeter of the former Arlington train station. The trail then passes Spy Pond, sparkling in the sunlight. This pond once provided the Boston area with much of its ice prior to modern refrigeration technology. The ice was harvested in the winter and stored in ice houses along the pond's shore until it was needed in warmer months.

After traveling 1 mile on the trail, you will see an interesting two-sided mileage stone marker, etched in Roman numerals, indicating the number of miles traveled from either end of the trail. These structures will be evident for the entire course.

In downtown Arlington, an array of shops and restaurants line the street. The majority of the buildings were erected in the 1950s.

The trail briefly joins Massachusetts Avenue. History buffs will want to stop at the Jefferson Cutter House, located in Whittemore Park in Arlington Center. Built in 1832, the completely restored home was donated to the Town of Arlington and in 1989 was moved to its current location. Listed on the National Register of Historical Places, the Cutter home sits at the original site of Arlington's town common. Take notice of the last remaining piece of railroad tracks of the Minuteman Bikeway located in front of the home.

The trail resumes near a statue of Sam Wilson. Born in Arlington in 1766, he later became America's national symbol, Uncle Sam. The trail passes the Arlington High school at the 2-mile mark, followed by the Bike Stop, which rents bikes and in-line skates.

For the next couple of miles the trail traverses several of Arlington's parks, culminating with the Arlington Reservoir and its summer swimming area, which converts to a winter skating pond. In Lexington, the Great Meadows park is particularly pretty with its 185 acres of wildflowers and wetland vegetation. The park was established as Arlington's watershed in 1873.

Trees line the Minuteman trail.

At mile marker 6, the trail cuts through Lexington Center. The former Lexington Center Station has gone through many transformations over the years. Most recently it was a bank, closing its doors in early 1999. New plans call for a historical museum to be located here.

Lexington is a beautiful town and is the perfect place to stop for a break. The town offers many places to eat and shop. The Lexington Visitor Center is adjacent to the trail. The center has an assortment of historical photos and information highlighting nearby Revolutionary-era sights, including a diorama of the Battle of Lexington Green. Historical photos of area depots are displayed here. Additional information regarding Lexington's conservation and bike trails are also available.

Passing through the train shed of the Lexington Center Station, the trail continues north. The highest point of the trail is at mile marker 7, which is 250 feet higher than the Alewife Station. At mile marker 8, the trail crosses busy Bedford Street at grade. Use caution.

Just beyond mile 8, the trail crosses over I–95 (also known as Route 128) on an overpass. There are several industrial and commercial developments at Hartwell Avenue. Again, use caution at this crossing, as it is quite active. A crossing signal will help you proceed safely.

The trail passes through a more wooded setting before reaching mile 10. Take a moment to view the photo at the Bedford Railroad Station illustrating an earlier version of the station in its heyday.

The trail ends about a half-mile later at South Street, where a bakery and bike and rental store are located in the former passenger station. The local historical society plans to renovate the railroad buildings to its original style. Plans include converting the older commuter passenger car next to the station into a railroad museum.

For more adventure go an additional 3 miles from Bedford to Billerica.

Other plans call for extending the trail 4 additional miles into Concord, where it would connect to the Minuteman National Historic Park. The National Park Service currently is working on plans to open a bike trail that would run the entire length of the park.

15 Northampton Bikeway

The town of Northampton is the home to prestigious Smith College and is known for its active community government. This short but sweet bikeway is an urban greenway that links downtown Northampton to spectacular Look Memorial Park.

Activities:

Location: Hampshire County

Length: 2.6 miles

Surface: Asphalt

Wheelchair access: Yes

Difficulty: Easy

Food: A number of restaurants are available in Northampton. Or consider packing a picnic lunch and enjoy eating it at Look Memorial Park.

Rest rooms: Look Memorial Park

Seasons: Open year-round.

Access and parking: Because the trail begins in the middle of a neighborhood with virtually no on-street parking, it is best to begin this trail in downtown Northampton. Take Main Street (Route 9) west past all of the shops and City Hall. Just before Routes 9 and 66 turn toward Williamsburg and Westhampton, take a right onto State Street and proceed 0.7 mile to the start of the trail. There is ample parking at Look Memorial Park as well.

Rentals: Northampton Bicycle, 319 Pleasant Street, Northampton, MA; (413) 586–3810.

Contact: Wayne Feiden, Director of Planning and Development, Northampton Office of Planning and Development, 210 Main Street, City Hall, Northampton, MA 01060-3110; (413) 586–6950; fax (413) 586–3726; wfeiden@city.northampton.ma.us.

• •

This is a perfect trail for people wanting to spend a short time in travel but a longer time exploring Northampton and nearby Look Memorial Park. It's recommended for families wanting a children-friendly park at the trail's end.

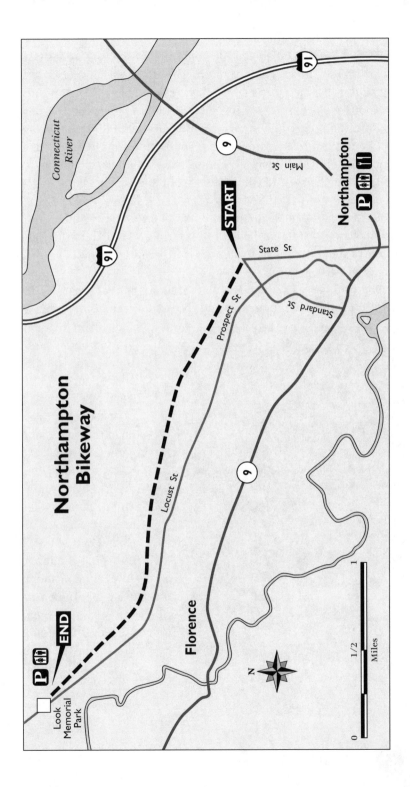

Parking is not available at the beginning of the trail, so it's best to park in downtown Northampton. This small city has been getting a lot of positive press lately. The residents of the community have done much to preserve the city's history. A popular tourist destination, the downtown area, which covers several blocks, brims with boutiques, restaurants, coffee shops, and trendy brew pubs. Take note of the architecturally interesting buildings, including the County Courthouse and the Academy of Music, which is the sixth-oldest theater in the United States.

From downtown Northampton take Main Street to State Street and proceed 0.7 mile to the start of the trail. The path to the right leads to a shopping plaza. To take the Northampton Bikeway to Look Memorial Park, go left.

The trail passes several Northampton residential areas. In the vicinity of mile marker 2, the path crosses a couple of streets at grade before heading into a wooded area filled with maple, willow, sumac, and beech trees.

At about 2.5 miles, the entrance to Look Memorial Park is visible to the left. This impeccably maintained park makes the short trail worthwhile. Here you will find picnic tables, playground, a swimming pool, tennis courts, paddle boat rentals, a concession stand, and a train ride for kids of all ages.

Local residents are the primary users of the trail.

One of Massachusetts' favorite rail-trails, the Norwottuck Rail-Trail is heavily used by commuting college students and by outdoor enthusiasts looking for a user-friendly trail.

Activities:

Location: Hampshire County

Length: 8.5 miles

Surface: Asphalt

Wheelchair access: Yes

Difficulty: Easy

Food: Restaurants are available in Amherst and Northampton.

Rest rooms: Elwell Recreation Area

Seasons: Open year-round.

Access and parking:

- *From I–91:* Take exit 19. Proceed straight at the end of the ramp onto Damon Road for about 1 block and then turn into Elwell State Park.
- *In Amherst:* Follow Route 9 to Southeast Street. Take a right. Proceed about 1 mile to a parking lot at the intersection of Mills Lane and Southeast Street. Additional parking is available by continuing for another mile to Station Road and taking a left to the parking lot.

Rentals:

- Northampton Bicycle, 319 Pleasant Street, Northampton, MA; (413) 586–3810.
- Bicycle World Too, 63 South Pleasant Street, Amherst, MA; (413) 253–7722.
- Competitive Edge, 374 Russell Street (Route 9), Hadley, MA; (413) 585–8833.
- The Elwell Recreation Area has a limited number of hand-cycles for wheelchair sports enthusiasts.

Transportation: The Pioneer Valley Transit Association offers public transportation in the area. Call (413) 785–1381 for more information.

Contact: Danny O'Brien, Department of Environmental Management, Division of Forests and Parks, 100 Cambridge Street, Boston, MA 02202; (617) 727–3180 or (800) 831–0569; www.magnet.state.ma.us/dem.htm.

H istorians believe that the Native Americans who first lived in the region named the area "Norwottuck," meaning "in the midst of the river."

The rail line originated as a Massachusetts Central Railroad route in 1887, opening after nearly twenty years of planning and construction. Stretching from Northampton to Boston, the route carried both freight and passengers including Calvin Coolidge, a Northampton native. The Boston & Maine Railroad eventually took over the line, although it had been plagued by financial problems. Passenger service on the line ended at the start of the Depression, but freight service continued on the line through 1980.

The State Department of Environmental Management purchased the line in 1985, two years after the tracks and ties were removed from the corridor. The agency converted the line into a rail-trail in the early 1990s and opened the trail to the public in 1993.

Almost immediately beyond the parking lot is the trail's most striking feature, a multitrestled bridge over New England's largest river, the Connecticut. The bridge spans more than a half-mile. Built in 1887, it is one of the few surviving iron bridges from that era. Below is Elwell Island, a 60-acre preserve that is home to more than a dozen species of birds. On the right is a bridge dedicated to Calvin Coolidge, who served as mayor of Northampton early in his political career, before becoming America's thirtieth president.

As the path resumes, take notice of the shimmering effect of the trail's surface. The "glass phalt" surface contains recycled crushed glass from Springfield. Also take note that the mileage markers begin at the Amherst start of the trail. If you park at Elwell Recreation Area the mile markers will begin at mile marker number 8 and decrease as you travel toward Amherst.

For the next 2 miles, the trail parallels Route 9 (on the right), with farmland lining the trail's left side and rolling hills in the background. Tobacco was once a dominant crop in this area and it is still grown in a few places. Dairy farms are also a primary industry in this part of Massachusetts. The trail crosses the historic Hadley Commons, an area once used by Hadley farmers whose animals grazed there. The former Hadley railroad station is standing on the south side of the trail, several hundred feet east of the Common.

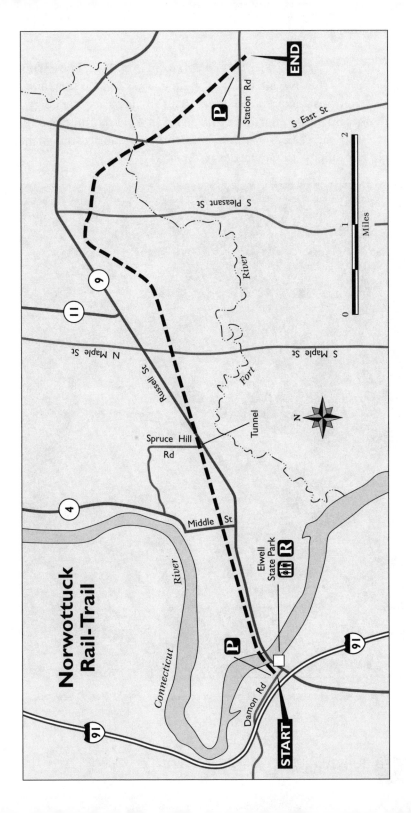

Norwottuck Rail-Trail

START

END

P

P

R

Station Rd

S East St

S Pleasant St

N Maple St

S Maple St

Russell St

River

Fort

Tunnel

Spruce Hill Rd

Middle St

Elwell State Park

Damon Rd

Connecticut River

River

9

11

4

91

9I

N

Miles

0   1   2

The trail crosses under Spruce Hill Road in a short, newly constructed box "tunnel" after passing mile marker 6. Soon thereafter, the trail crosses under Russell Street (Route 9) using another culvert with no sight lines to the other side; use caution. After mile marker 5, the trail passes behind Hampshire and Mountains Farms Malls and a few other commercial developments.

The half-mile bridge spanning the Connecticut River is a highlight of the Norwottuck Rail-Trail.

By the trail's midpoint (near mile marker 4), the trail becomes a quiet tunnel of young trees—including oak, maple, and white birch—while thousands of wild ferns cloak the forest floor. The trail becomes progressively more rural, although the Amherst Golf Course does border the trail prior to mile marker 3. A large grassy area with a picnic table is located just past the golf course.

As the trail nears downtown Amherst, ramps provide direct access to Route 116 (Pleasant Street). Amherst College is located on the

Dense woods surround much of the Norwottuck Rail-Trail.

left, near mile marker 2. Continuing east, dense woods overtake the trail's perimeter before crossing over the Fort River and South East Street on two short bridges. Much of the surrounding area is owned by the college or the Town of Amherst and is designated as conservation land. There are several hiking trails worth exploring through the swampy area.

Wetlands are visible along the trail's left side in the vicinity of mile marker 1, and a large mix of birds—including herons and meadowlarks—enjoy the surroundings. Soon the trail reaches Station Road, where the paved trail ends at a large parking lot. The trail continues undeveloped for another 1.3 miles, although it will be paved in the future. In addition, at the trail's western end, plans call for connecting the Norwottuck Rail-Trail with the Northampton Bikeway.

17 Southwest Corridor

This urban rail-trail takes you from downtown Boston to Jamaica Plain. It is used by bicyclists commuting to and from downtown and by outdoor enthusiasts looking for some fun in the sun near Boston.

Activities:

Location: Suffolk County

Length: 5 miles

Surface: Asphalt

Wheelchair access: Yes

Difficulty: Easy

Food: Restaurants and fast food shops are close by throughout the length of this trail. The trail passes through the South End of Boston, Roxbury, and Jamaica Plain, where there are food establishments aplenty.

Rest rooms: The Back Bay T Station and Forest Hill T Station have public rest rooms.

Seasons: Open year-round.

Access and parking: Parking in the Back Bay or South End areas of Boston is difficult unless you enter a parking lot and pay upwards to $20 for the time spent on the trail. You may want to consider taking the "T" to either the Back Bay station on the Orange Line of the MBTA (Massachusetts Bay Transit Authority) or take a commuter rail or Amtrak train to the Back Bay stop. You can bring a bike on the T by showing a Bike Pass ($5.00 buys a pass for four years). Bike passes are available at the Special Pass Office (617–722–5438) at the Downtown Crossing station on weekdays.

Rentals:
- Back Bay Bikes and Boards, 336 Newbury, Boston, MA; (617) 247–2336.
- Community Bicycle Supply, 496 Tremont, Boston, MA; (617) 542–8623.
- Ferris Wheels Bicycle Shop, 64 South Street, Jamaica Plain, MA; (617) 522–7082.
- Jamaica Cycle and Sports, 667 Centre Street, Jamaica Plain, MA; (617) 524–9610.

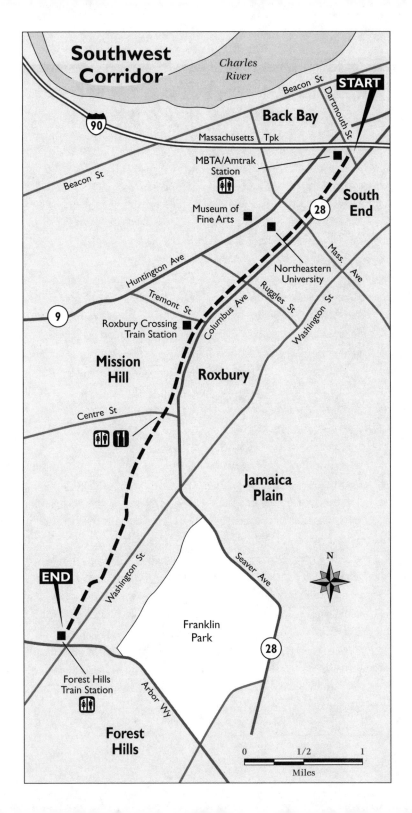

CREATING THE SOUTHWEST CORRIDOR PARK

In the 1950s and 1960s, many transportation experts believed that the best solution to growing traffic congestion was to build larger highways. Boston city planners, who had been eyeing a Penn-Central right-of-way since 1948, unveiled a master plan that called for an elevated eight-lane expressway. This extension of I-95 would run into downtown Boston, through Jamaica Plain and Roxbury, with a rapid-transit line down the center. A connecting highway, the Inner Belt, would veer off into Cambridge.

Aghast, Cambridge residents were the first group in the city to form an antihighway movement in 1966. Soon, Jamaica Plain residents, not expecting to stop the highway, began lobbying for one below-grade. By 1969, however, the times were changing. Protest demonstrations at the State House persuaded Governor Francis Sargent to declare a moratorium on all highway construction in Boston, and—after intense lobbying from all sides—he canceled the Southwest Expressway in 1972. Instead, a new rapid-transit line was planned for the corridor, to replace the noisy elevated rapid transit on nearby Washington Street.

The local communities had won, which was the first step in creating the Southwest Corridor Park. The community-based coalition that had fought against the highway formed a nonprofit coalition in 1974 to help plan and design the park and rapid-transit station. Each neighborhood formed a task force to focus on its section of the 52-acre park. Community members were involved in all aspects of the park and transit corridor design.

The citizens' concerns were incorporated into the final design, in the form of grade separation, barriers, and better street access. Funding was scarce during much of the development and an $80 million shortfall in 1982 did not help matters. The entire project, including the railroad and transit tunnel, the eight T stations, street reconstruction, and park development cost $750 million.

Today it is hard to imagine that Southwest Corridor Park—a multifaceted, urban greenway that provides transportation choices and recreation opportunities for hundreds of thousands of people—began as a soot-covered, out-of-commission urban wasteland. The result has been well worth the investment.

Contact: Allan Morris, Parkland Manager, Southwest Corridor Park, 38 New Heath Street, Jamaica Plain, MA 02130; (617) 727–0057.

• •

The Southwest Corridor is a tribute to the tenacity of outdoor enthusiasts who persisted until the trail became a reality. It is built over five active rail lines: two rapid transit and three Amtrak and commuter lines.

It took hundreds of community participants twenty years of demonstrating, lobbying, and meeting with officials to turn an unsightly old railroad corridor into a landscaped linear park. The Southwest Corridor Park continues a long tradition of creating open spaces and recreational sites in the Greater Boston area, dating back to 1893, when the state set aside nearly 10,000 acres of land for green space. Today, although the metropolitan areas seem more congested than ever, the parks and paths remains an invaluable natural resource.

Until recently, however, one area had lacked open space: the neighborhoods lying southwest of downtown, including Forest Hills, Roxbury, Jamaica Plain, and the South End. In fact, until the 1980s, an active railroad ran on a granite embankment through the area, dividing one neighborhood from the other.

After an attempt to turn the route into an eight-lane highway failed, this once-blighted corridor has been transformed into a 5-mile linear park with two paths, eight rapid transit stations, and nearly a dozen community gardens. Along a corridor that now unites a

Community gardens line the trail.

number of multiethnic communities, you find numerous basketball courts, tennis courts, and works of art—not to mention two
fountains and two street hockey rinks. With so much packed into
5 miles, it's no wonder the Southwest Corridor Park has won several awards since its 1988 opening. Plan to spend some time exploring the trail and the many historic sites nearby.

The trail begins in a small plaza on Dartmouth Street, just across
from the Back Bay/South End MBTA/Amtrak station. While gazing

City dwellers enjoy outdoor fun on the trail.

at the huge archway into the station, look beyond it for a view of the John Hancock Building, a giant, glass-covered parallelogram. To the left is Tent City, a mixed-income housing development that won the 1994 World Habitat Award. Passing through the plaza, the brick path indicates the beginning of the corridor. A map on a pillar will orient you to the path.

The first half-mile of the park winds through the South End, past row houses, quiet side streets, landscaped terraces, and balcony gardens. Soon you see Boston's other showpiece skyscraper, the Prudential Building, off to the right on Boylston Street. Also of interest is the domed First Church of Christ, Scientist, which is the world headquarters for the Christian Science Church. Soon the path intersects with Massachusetts Avenue. "Mass Ave." is the only intersection along the corridor that is not bike-friendly. Your best bet, if you are on a bicycle, is to dismount and walk across the street. The trail resumes on the left side of the Massachusetts Avenue T Station.

Soon the path enters the working-class neighborhood of Roxbury. Notice that the path splits in two: one for bicycling and the other for foot traffic. This dual path design is intended to increase use and minimize conflicts between faster-moving cyclists and other users. Shortly, the trail passes near the first of many vegetable and flower gardens cared for by about 150 community gardeners.

After another block the path appears to dead-end across from a large playing field and tennis courts. Turn left onto the street and right onto a wide sidewalk at the next block, Columbus Avenue. Signs for the Southwest Corridor Park appear after a few hundred feet, just after passing the field and a Northeastern University parking lot.

The giant entryway arch of the Ruggles Street T Station rises in front of you. One of the eight rapid transit stations that opened in 1987, this one has a vaulted interior. Next, you arrive at four monoliths, which—through handwritten letters—tell stories of different Boston immigrants who once lived on Ruggles Street.

At Ruggles Street, a pillar depicts a trail map and a short history of Roxbury. Settled in 1630, it is the center of Boston's African-American community. During the 1860s, Roxbury was a major stop on the underground railroad for escaping slaves and later it became a meeting place for the newly formed NAACP. Dr. Martin Luther King Jr. preached at his home church in Roxbury while studying at Boston University.

To the right of the trail, located several blocks away but worthy of a visit, are two Boston treasures: the Museum of Fine Arts and the Isabella Stewart Gardner Museum.

The next stretch of the path has a small amphitheater, basketball courts, and a good view of the rapid-transit lines—sunken behind a triple row of border trees. In fact, one-quarter of the park is decked over the railroad tracks, providing more space for grass, plantings, and recreational facilities.

At the Roxbury Crossing T Station on Tremont Street are several large archival photographs. On the hill to the right is the recently restored Mission Hill Basilica, the namesake of the Mission Hill neighborhood. To the left, on Tremont Street, is Roxbury Community College and the new Reggie Lewis Track and Athletic Center, built in memory of the up-and-coming Boston Celtics player who died suddenly in 1991.

The next three T stations along the Southwest Park (Jackson Square, Stony Brook, and Green Street) are located in Jamaica Plain, a lively, multicultural area. At the brick-facaded Jackson Square Station, you can take a right to Centre Street, passing an assortment of restaurants before reaching the center of Jamaica Plain.

The trail ends at the Forest Hills T Station. Take note of the minimalist clock tower at the station—a landmark for the southern end of the park

From here, you can make a short extension of the Southwest Corridor Park to the left and then along a parkway to reach Franklin Park and the Franklin Park Zoo. (A map of the area is outside the Forest Hills T Station.) You can also reach the Arnold Arboretum by picking up the path along the right side of the Forest Hills station. Cross onto South Street at a stoplight, and at the bottom of a short hill is the gated entrance to the arboretum.

MORE TRAVELS WITH CYNTHIA

by Holly Mascott Nadler

t's not my sister Cynthia's fault that every time we schedule a bicycling trip together, something goes wrong. I'm not above considering the possibility that some sort of jinx hovers over our outings. Maybe we picked up a nasty but not completely debilitating voodoo hex on a long-ago trip to New Orleans. Whatever the reason, the fact remains that every time we've agreed to pack up our bikes and head for a good trail, there's a glitch at the start.

Take, for instance, the time we decided to bike from Wood's Hole to Falmouth. This short seaside ride was the smallest part of our planned trek, for the more elaborate portion of our itinerary involved Cindy's coming to Martha's Vineyard to headquarter at my house before we took off for bigger adventures the next day.

On the appointed morning we bicycled 3 miles to Vineyard Haven to catch the ferry, only to be informed (this was in late June when the throngs start to implode around any well-laid plan) that there'd be no guaranteed room for our bikes on the next ferry. The reason: too many cars with reserved spaces. A slightly tense exchange took place as the bicycle-blissed-out Mascott sisters argued that the more bikes employed as transportation to and from the island, the less traffic we'd all endure and the happier life would be for everyone concerned, so why should the Steamship Authority ever seek to restrict space for trim little vehicles in favor of fat, clunky, internal-combustion, smog-making vehicles? The clerk, unfortunately, was indifferent to our plea for a two-wheeled society and we had to remind ourselves that policy was never set by the people behind the front desk. We turned on our heels and raced like crazy to the next ferry leaving Oak Bluffs, roughly 3 miles away. We missed it.

"Are we having fun yet?" Cindy asked as we sank wearily—hours later—onto a hard vinyl bench on the foredeck.

Actually we were. We always enjoy ourselves, even on those trips where, in keeping with the Mascott bicycling curse, our bikes sit in the shed of a quaint bed and breakfast, rain pouring down, as we sip hot chocolate by the fire and scan the movie page in the local paper. On an autumn biking trip to the Sandwich area, for instance, an unannounced storm sidelined our bikes but made it possible for us to visit four—count 'em—four Christmas Tree Shops in the space of six hours. Another time in Provincetown, nor'easter winds propelled us from coffee shop to boutique, our bikes never once leaving the car rack.

The important thing is to keep on trying, keep on making plans, because when we do hit a sunny stretch of bike path through a sylvan wood or astride a silver-dotted sea, we know we've lucked into one of the most pleasurable activities in life, made all the more wonderful when shared with your sister.

MORE RAIL-TRAILS

① Lowell Canalway

Although on the register of rail trails, the Lowell Canalway is not your typical rail-trail. This "trail" is a waterway that can be sampled by a boat ride through the canals that were once the arteries of the industrial revolution in Lowell.

Activities: By tour only

Location: Middlesex County

Length: 3.5 miles, with an additional 2 miles to be completed in the future

Wheelchair access: Yes

Food: The Lowell National Historic Park has a small restaurant. There are numerous restaurants in the city of Lowell.

Rest rooms: Available at the Lowell National Historical Park

Seasons: Open daily during the summer and on weekends from early May to July and from September to Columbus Day.

Access and parking: Take the Lowell Connector from either Route 495 (exit 35A) or Route 3 (exit 30A) to Thorndike Street (exit 5B). Follow the brown-and-white park signs to the parking lot. Parking is free at the visitor parking lot next to Market Mills.

Rentals: None

Transportation: Train service is available from Boston. Call the Massachusetts Bay Transportation Authority at (617) 222–3200 or contact them through their Web site at www.mbta.com.

Contact: Christina Briggs, Lowell National Historical Park; (978) 275–1725.

The Lowell Canalway is a testament to the tenacity of Lowell residents seeking to improve their city through the development of a chain of parks following the old canals of the city. In the nineteenth century, Lowell was one of the leading New England industrial cities. In 1822 the Merrimack Manufacturing Company began constructing mills and digging a network of power canals. Driven by water, machines were able to spin thread from cotton

In Lowell's heyday, a labyrinth of train tracks and canals connected its mills.

and made cloth from the thread. During its heyday in the 1850s, Lowell was the largest cotton textile center in the nation. At the end of the nineteenth century, Lowell experienced a decline when much of the textile manufacturers moved to the American South. By the mid-twentieth century, Lowell was severely economically depressed. Efforts to revitalize Lowell were spearheaded in 1974 by native-born Congressman Paul Tsongas. In 1977, community leaders were able to have Congress approve the creation of the Lowell National Historic Park.

The Lowell Canalway passes through Lowell's downtown area. At the Mack Plaza, a park trolley stop and display area contains a Victorian garden and is the display area for the Boston & Maine rolling stock, once the site of the original terminus of the Boston & Lowell Railroad. Much of the canal follows existing railroad rights-of-way.

The Canalway tour begins at the Trolley Swamp Locks. Guided by park rangers, the boat will take you past the Pawtucket Locks at Frances Gate to the Merrimack River. The boats then pass the Northern Canal Lock to the Suffolk Mills where a water power exhibit is featured. A trolley then takes passengers back to the original site.

J Quarries Footpath

A quick jaunt to a granite quarry for history buffs and sightseers.

Activities:

Location: Norfolk

Length: 0.5 mile

Surface: Dirt

Wheelchair access: No

Difficulty: Easy

Food: Quincy has a full spectrum of restaurants.

Rest rooms: None

Seasons: Open year-round.

Access and parking: To get to the Quarries, take I–93 to Furnace Brook Parkway. Follow signs to Willard Street. At the bottom of the ramp turn left and cross under the Expressway. Take the first right onto Ricciuti Drive. The Quincy Quarries is 0.25 mile on the right.

Rentals: None

Contact: Maggie Brown, Quincy Quarries Historical Site, Blue Hills Reservation; (617) 698–1802.

• •

The Quincy Quarries were the source of the granite used to build the Bunker Hill Monument in Charlestown. The Granite Railway was built in 1826 to carry stone from the quarries. For the next 140 years, over fifty quarries operated in Quincy. The town was nicknamed "The Granite City." The last active quarry closed in 1963. The railway has been included in the registry of National Historic Civil Engineering Landmarks.

The trail is only a half-mile long. Of special interest is the Granite Railway Incline, located off Mullin Avenue. A young engineer, Gridley Bryant, designed and constructed the structure four years after the railway was built. The granite was moved in specially built cars from the upland quarries down to the level of the main railway, a vertical drop of 84 feet.

Group tours are available highlighting the quarries' natural and cultural history. For more information, contact the Quincy Quarries Historical Site at the Blue Hills Reservation at (617) 698–1802.

Future Massachusetts Rail-Trails

Massachusetts has a large number of rail-trail projects in the works. Be on the lookout for the development of the East Boston Greenway, an abandoned railroad corridor that will connect the marshes, beaches, playing fields, Logan Airport, MBTA stations, and residential areas throughout the East Boston community.

The Neponset River Greenway includes a railroad right-of-way that extends from the harbor in Dorchester to Central Avenue in Milton. It is currently almost usable, but the railroad ballast makes it very rough going from the Old Colony railroad bridge in Port Norfolk (access under the Hancock Street bridge) to Central Avenue. The trail will link several parks along the Neponset Estuary, and will also connect with the MDC's harbor path.

The Bedford Narrow-Gauge Rail-Trail is a 3-mile-long stone-dust right-of-way that will run from the end of the Minuteman Bikeway in Bedford to Billerica. The trail now ends at the Bedford/Billerica town line at Route 3.

The Assabet River Rail-Trail is a planned 12-mile bike and pedestrian path on a long-abandoned railroad right-of-way paralleling the Assabet River through Hudson, Stow, and Maynard, with connections to Marlborough and a commuter rail station in South Acton.

The Bike to the Sea Trail will run from the center of Malden through Everett to Revere Beach, Saugus, Lynn, and Nahant. This 10-mile-long path will include urban and open space along the Saugus Branch Railroad. Following the Malden River to North Revere and past Rumney Marsh, the trail will then run along the Saugus River and marshes and head toward the Lynn and Nahant beaches. The Bike to the Sea Trail is part of the East Coast Greenway plan.

West from the end of the proposed Wayside Rail-Trail in Berlin, the Central Massachusetts Line parallels U.S. 20 through Waltham, Weston, Wayland, and Sudbury, then heads northwest through Hudson and Berlin to Clinton. Plans call for the trail to continue across the middle of the state, south around the Quabbin Reservoir, and then to Amherst.

The Cochituate Rail-Trail will use the Saxonville Branch Line roadbed to provide downtown Natick a recreational route north along Lake Cochituate and to the day-use area of Cochituate State Park. The northern extension, along the west bank of Cochituate Brook and up to Route 126 at the Sudbury River, will provide the same access from north of the Massachusetts Turnpike.

The Dedham Rail-Trail will utilize the abandoned rail line from the Readville Station in Boston past Dedham High School and almost to Route 1. The trail is being considered as part of Dedham's open space plan.

The Lowell-Sudbury (Bruce Freeman) Trail will convert the Old Colony rail line from Framingham to Lowell into a multiuse trail. Running through Sudbury, Concord, Acton, Westford, and Chelmsford, it will connect to the Minuteman Commuter Bikeway Extension in Acton and the Central Massachusetts bike path in Sudbury, and will terminate at the Merrimac River in Lowell.

If you'd like to volunteer to work on one or two of these future trails, you can contact Steve Wilson (781–381–7711, extension 102) for details on the Bike to the Sea Trail or Alan Trench (978–470–1982) for information about the Bay Circuit.

Rails-to-Trails

NEW HAMPSHIRE

New Hampshire

18 Ashuelot Rail-Trail
19 Mason Rail-Trail
20 Rockingham Recreational Trail (Portsmouth Branch)
21 Sugar River Recreational Trail

K Fremont Trail
L Hillsborough Trail
M Wolfeboro-Sanbornville Recreational Trail
N Zealand Recreation Area

MAINE

Berlin

N

VERMONT

NEW
HAMPSHIRE

Concord

Manchester

Nashua

MASSACHUSETTS

INTRODUCTION

I n many ways, New Hampshire is two states—southern New Hampshire and northern New Hampshire. Southern New Hampshire hugs the Massachusetts border, and for many people the close proximity to Boston lures them to that portion of the state. New companies have moved into southern New Hampshire, boosting the economy.

Southern New Hampshire is graced with lakes and forests. Portsmouth, on the coast, has preserved much of its charm and historical beauty. Wander through downtown Portsmouth, where many buildings date to Colonial times, or through adjacent neighborhoods, where wonderful homes were built by sea captains in the nineteenth century. Also of note is the town of Fitzwilliam, which has retained much of its original grace. Its building span three centuries, and antiques shops line the downtown streets. The nearby Rhododendron State Forest offers a feast for the eyes during the summer when flowers are in bloom.

Concord and Manchester are the largest cities. Concord is the capital and the state's major industrial and political center. Manchester was once a thriving textile mill town, employing thousands of workers. It fell on hard times when many textile companies moved south, but local business leaders have launched a campaign to revive the center city.

Travel north in New Hampshire and lakes and mountains dominate the scenery. Here you will find such gems as Lake Winnipesaukee, Sunapee Lake, and Mirror Lake. The White Mountains—the highest peaks in New England—are the state's jewel in the crown. Adventurous souls may wish to climb all 6,288 feet of Mt. Washington. Or consider taking a three-hour round trip tour to the summit on the Mt. Washington Cog Railway, open daily in summer.

New Hampshire's rail-trails offer you a chance to explore the state's beauty. Especially pleasing is the Ashuelot Rail-Trail, which takes you past the Ashuelot River and through pretty farmland. The Sugar River Recreational Trail has more than a dozen bridges, including a pair of covered bridges designed more than a century ago by master woodworkers. North, in the White Mountain region, the Zealand Recreation Area offers hikers the chance to climb several trails, including the Sugarloaf Trail, the Hale Brook Trail, the Zealand Trail, and the Trestle Trail.

TOP RAIL-TRAILS

18 Ashuelot Rail-Trail

This charming 21-mile trail is very pretty and well worth exploring. It passes by the Ashuelot River and through New Hampshire farm country.

Activities:

Location: Cheshire County

Length: 21 miles

Surface: The surface is sandy at times until it reaches Keene State University, where the trail is much better maintained.

Wheelchair access: Limited. Wheelchairs will fare well at the end of the trail near Keene State University. The going will be much more difficult farther from the university, where the surface is sandy and poorly maintained.

Difficulty: Moderate

Food: Several eateries are available in the small town of Winchester and at the Keene State University campus.

Rest rooms: Rest rooms are available on the Keene State University campus at the end of the trail.

Seasons: Open year-round.

Access and parking: From I–91 proceed north until you reach Route 10 (exit 28). Take a right and continue 15 miles until you reach Route 119. Turn left onto Route 119 west for about 6 miles, then turn left onto Route 63 south. Watch your odometer. When you have driven 2.2 miles, you will be at Dole Junction, which is not marked. Parking is available here, however, on the right side of the road. The trail begins on the opposite side of the street.

Rentals: None

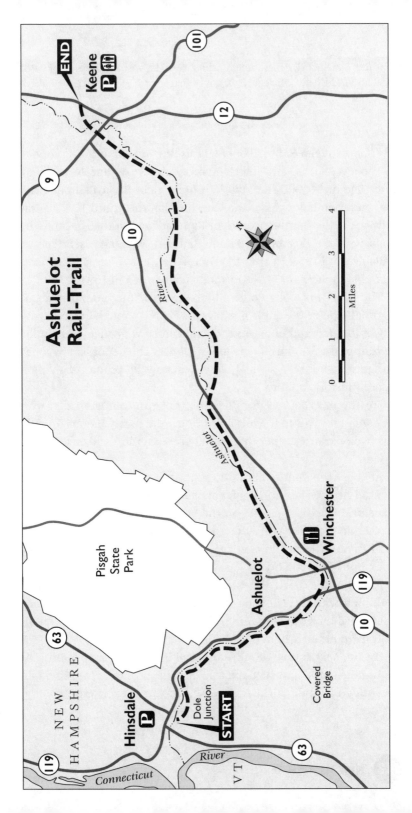

Contact: Bob Spoerl, Program Specialist, New Hampshire Division of Parks and Recreation, Trails Bureau, P.O. Box 495, Concord, NH 03302-1856; (603) 271–2629.

· ·

The Ashuelot Railroad opened this line in 1851, offering service between East Northfield in Massachusetts to Keene, New Hampshire. The line was owned by the Connecticut River Railroad until 1860 and then belonged to the Cheshire Railroad until 1877. It was sold back to the Connecticut River Railroad, and in 1893 became the property of the Boston and Maine Railroad. Passenger service was available until 1953. In 1977 the Green Mountain Railroad took over the rights to the line. It was formally abandoned in 1983.

The trail runs along Route 63 for about the first mile past farms on either side of the trail. The terrain is pretty rough at the beginning of the trail and in places the path can be very soggy. At 1 mile, the trail passes the former Ashuelot Depot. The depot is now a private home. There are several old boxcars on the property, giving it a quaint historic quality.

For the next couple of miles, the trail runs along a ridge with the Ashuelot River to the left, affording quite pretty views. You will pass two operating paper mills where several more old boxcars can be seen.

At about the 4-mile mark, the trail passes through the Ashuelot Covered Bridge (Route 119), which is listed in the National Register of Historic Places. A plaque on the bridge reads, $5.00 FINE FOR RIDING OR DRIVING OVER THE BRIDGE FASTER THAN A WALK.

At the 5-mile mark, the trail becomes quite sandy before crossing an iron and wood bridge.

At the 7-mile mark, the trail crosses a small road. There's a sign on the left with directions to Winchester. The town is a nice place to stop for lunch or sightseeing. To get to Winchester, take a left off the trail and then a right onto Route 10.

For the next couple of miles the trail is relatively uneventful. At the 10-mile mark, however, the trail crosses the Dino's Crossing railroad bridge. At mile 11 the trail passes by Monadnack Spring on the left, and at mile 12 it crosses Keene Road heading toward Swanzey, New Hampshire.

This may be a good place to turn around as the trail is generally in poor shape from this point on. It is sandy in some places and narrow. The trail runs very close to private homes along this stretch. At mile 17, the trail crosses another iron bridge. Once over the bridge, the trail is in much better shape again, as it approaches the campus of Keene State University. Many students use the trail for jogging or walking. The trail runs along the Keene State Athletic field until it ends on the campus.

The Ashuelot Covered Bridge.

A tour of lush New England forest on the border of New Hampshire and Massachusetts.

Activities:

Location: Hillsborough County

Length: 6.7 miles

Surface: Sand and gravel

Wheelchair access: No

Difficulty: Easy for pedestrians, but moderate to difficult for cyclists due to the sandy surface.

Food: None

Rest rooms: None

Seasons: Open year-round.

Access and parking: From I–495, take exit 31 and turn right onto Route 225. It will turn into Route 119 after about 10 miles. Continue northwest on Route 119 to Townsend, Massachusetts. Continue west toward West Townsend for less than 2 miles, turning right at the sign for Mason, New Hampshire. In 1.5 miles, bear right at the fork onto Greenville Road and proceed 1 mile to the Massachusetts/New Hampshire border. A gravel parking lot is located on the left side of the road. To get to the trail, turn right on Morse Road and travel uphill for 0.3 mile. Bear left, where you will see an orange gate leading to the trailhead.

Rentals:

• Happy Day Cycle, 237 South Street, Milford, NH; (603) 673–5088.

• Absolutely Bicycles, North Road, New Ipswitch, NH; (603) 878–4059.

Contact: Liz Fletcher, Commissioner, Mason Conservation Commission, Mann House, Darling Hill Road, Mason, NH 03048; (603) 878–2070.

• •

Looking for forest and wildlife? Then look no farther. The area on the border between New Hampshire and Massachusetts is New England outdoors at its best.

The original railroad line, which later became a branch of the

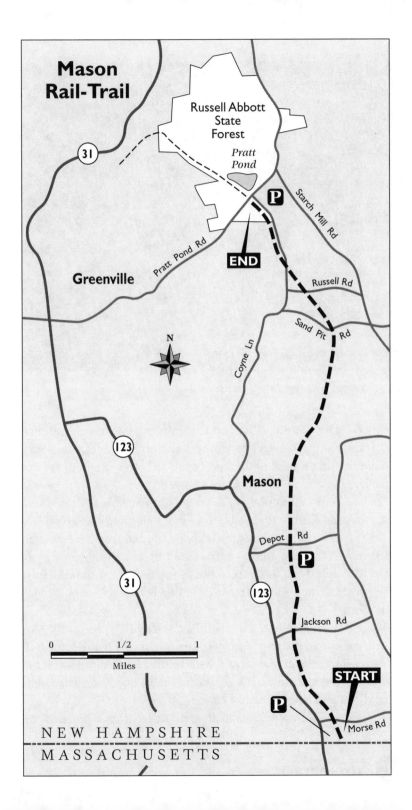

A small wooden bridge on the Mason Rail-Trail.

Boston & Maine Railroad, served the granite industry in southern New Hampshire. Passenger service was also offered on the line. Business on the line waned in the late 1950s, although the line was not officially abandoned until the late 1970s.

As you begin the trail, look to your right to catch a glimpse of a small waterfall before the trail curves gradually into the woods. An occasional railroad tie crosses the trail and sporadic rocks jut through the surface. Soon the trail is surrounded by a lush forest of pine, oak, and maple, with birch trees occasionally thrown into the mix. Rocky embankments, often covered with wild ferns, line both sides of the trail.

After the 1-mile marker, the path heads slightly uphill as the surface becomes more hard packed. At approximately 1.5 miles, the trail crosses over Jackson Street on a high bridge. Scores of large stone blocks support the bridge. Once across the bridge, the surface has some erosion problems, so use caution.

In another half-mile, the trail crosses Depot Road. While no remnants of the depot remain, the building most likely sat on the right side of the corridor, which is now a parking lot for the trail. The trail continues uphill for the next couple of miles. Some relics of the granite industry exist in this area, primarily in the form of granite slabs in the trail's vicinity.

At the 4-mile marker, fragrant pines and fir trees line the trail's right side while oaks shroud most of the rocky mounds on the left. After crossing Sand Pit Road, the trail gets quite sandy and begins to narrow. A tiny footbridge carries you over side-by-side ponds connected by a creek. The trail then traverses a sandy hill and crosses another bridge (with wide spaces between the planks). The trail levels out before crossing Russell Road. Take a break at the edge of the pines and watch the birds that have made the area their home.

The trail continues its straight path on the other side of Russell Road and mature trees cover the trail. Around the 5-mile mark the trail crosses Wilton Avenue and parallels it for about a half-mile. The trails leads uphill, crosses under a set of power lines, then veers away from the road. At this point, state forest land lines the left side.

Near mile 6 is Pratt Pond, the highlight of the trail. Jagged rock formations outline the edge of the pond above pockets of white pine interspersed with the occasional maple. In the summer many

Mountain bicyclists enjoy the rugged surface of the Mason Rail-Trail.

wildflowers bloom here and later in the year the area seems aflame with the fall colors for which New England is famous.

The trail follows Pratt Pond for about a half-mile before it returns to state forest land. The pond was donated by the descendants of the Russell and Abbot families as a "joint family memorial" to two of the oldest families in Wilton and Mason. The pond once supplied water power to the nearby starch mill and is currently a favorite spot for warm-water fishing and canoeing enthusiasts.

The managed section of the trail ends 7 miles from where it started; however, the corridor continues (with a few obstructions) for another 2 miles. In this section, the trail curves west before turning south toward Greenville.

The trail ends where a massive bridge once spanned the valley into Greenville. The stone supports for the railroad bridge still stand, towering almost 60 feet in the air. These structures are a striking reminder of the region's railroad heritage.

The end of the Mason Rail-Trail, where a bridge once spanned the valley.

Edged by two lakes, a river, and a pond, this pretty trail is defined by water. It's New Hampshire at its best.

Activities:

Location: Rockingham County

Length: 25.5 miles

Surface: Gravel and original ballast

Wheelchair access: Limited

Difficulty: Moderate

Food: A full array of eateries are available in nearby Manchester, Epping, and Raymond.

Rest rooms: None

Seasons: Open year-round.

Access and parking: From Manchester, take exit 7 off I–93 onto Route 101 east. Almost immediately, take exit 1 off Route 101 and take a right onto southbound Route 28. You will soon reach a traffic rotary. Continue on Route 28 through the rotary, and just past the rotary turn left into a parking lot at Lake Massabesic. If the lot is full or closed, park at one of the turn-offs on Route 28 across from the lake.

Rentals:

- Bike Barn, Too, 14 East Broadway, Derry, NH; (603) 432–7907.
- Cycles Etceteras, 13 Range Road, Salem, NH; (603) 890–3212.
- Flying Wheels, 450 South Broadway, Salem, NH; (603) 893–0225.
- Merrimack Bicycle Shop, 1 Pinkerton Street, Derry, NH; (603) 437–0277.

Contact: Paul Gray, Chief Bureau of Trails, Division of Parks and Recreation, 172 Pembroke Road, P.O. Box 1865, Concord, NH 03302-1856; (603) 271–3254; fax (603) 271–2629.

• •

Manchester, the largest city in New Hampshire, boasts a long, well-maintained rail-trail just outside the city limits. This 25-mile corridor, once part of the extensive Boston & Maine Railroad network, runs one-third of the way across the state, ending just a few miles from the Atlantic Ocean.

This section of the Boston & Maine Railroad corridor, called the Portsmouth Branch, originally served the textile industry—back when Manchester's mills made this city the home of the textile revolution. The Portsmouth Branch of the Rockingham Recreational Trail was opened to the public in 1991.

Travelers should be aware that this isn't the only trail in the area known as the Rockingham Recreational Trail. A few miles south, there is a 14-mile trail of the same name running from Windham Depot to Fremont. This shorter trail is actually the original Rockingham Recreational Trail, created in the mid-1980s mainly to accommodate the growing popularity of snowmobiles, all-terrain vehicles, and motorized dirt-bikes. The New Hampshire Bureau of Trails currently is working to link the two Rockingham trails to each other and to a third trail to create a large triangular trail network in southeastern New Hampshire.

Departing from the western terminus, the rail-trail follows the shoreline of Lake Massabesic. This lake sparkles in the sunlight and sailboats dot the horizon. There are many popular hiking and biking trails in the area. Trails that branch off to the right from the "Rock Rec" lead to this network of trails. At approximately the 3-mile mark on this rail-trail, another network of trails can be accessed near Tower Hill Pond. The trail then approaches a tunnel. It is quite sandy inside the tunnel, so use caution.

At the 5-mile mark, the trail reaches a tunnel underneath Route 101. A half-mile farther is another tunnel. The tunnels are similar: Each is uphill and covered with rocks and sand on both sides. It's a little treacherous to approach the tunnels and then go downhill after leaving them. The landscape now settles into a long stretch of quiet woods of pine, birch, and oaks. After another 4 miles, the site of the former East Candia Railroad Station will appear on the left, just before an intersection with a paved road. This is a good place to begin a shorter trip along the rail-trail.

Beyond the depot, the corridor becomes more secluded as it approaches Onway Lake. The trail and land near Onway Lake are privately owned, with nonmotorized access permitted. Be sure to pass with consideration and to respect the wishes of the local owners.

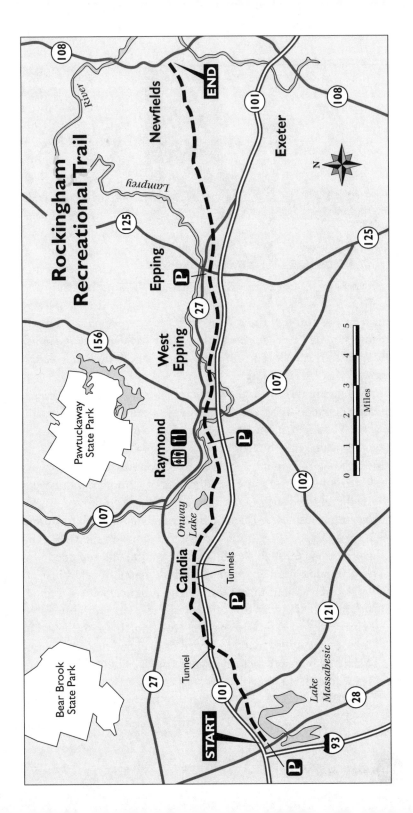

The trail follows the shoreline of scenic Lake Massabesic.

The rail-trail takes on several interesting features once it passes beyond the lake. It first runs along an elevated stretch through deep woods. It then passes through a granite cut and, at mile 12, enters another short tunnel. At around the trail's halfway point it passes through the quaint town of Raymond. Take a break here to rest or eat. You can also explore some of the handsome buildings, such as the restored railroad station, which now houses the Raymond Historical Society.

After leaving the town, the trail crosses a large railroad bridge. The next intersection is a rural highway near Route 101, with a mall-like stretch of department stores. Soon, however, the trail is back in the woods again with the Lamprey River appearing on the right.

In the town of Epping, the trail crosses another rural highway. This is also where the original Rockingham Trail from Fremont eventually will join this trail when a bridge crossing is improved.

Continuing east toward Newfields, the trail has a few bumpy and rutted spots. A speedway track and grandstand is on the right. The last several miles through Newfields are tranquil and secluded.

The trail ends at an abandoned railroad depot, located just off Route 108, about a half-mile north of the junction with Route 85. At this point you are just a few miles south of lively Durham, home to the University of New Hampshire. Head north on Route 108 to Durham, or go south to reach the town of Exeter. One of the country's oldest and most prestigious private schools, Philip Exeter Academy, is located in this town.

Think rivers and streams and a dozen bridges. The Sugar River Recreational Trail is a wonderland of forest treasures.

Activities:

Location: Sullivan County

Length: 10 miles

Surface: Gravel and original ballast

Wheelchair access: None

Difficulty: Moderately difficult for cyclists due to the sandy conditions of the trail.

Food: At the end of the trail, take Route 103 into Claremont, where several restaurants are located.

Rest rooms: None

Seasons: Open year-round.

Access and parking: From I–89, take exit 9 to Route 103 and turn left, passing the towns of Bradford and Newbury, and Sunapee Lake, before entering Newport. Head north on Route 101 for 0.25 mile past the town green and turn left onto Belknap Avenue. A well-marked parking lot is located on the right.

Rentals:

- Bob Skinner's Bike Shop, Route 103, Mt. Sunapee, NH; (603) 763–2303.
- Claremont Cyclesport, 32 Tremont Square, Claremont, NH; (603) 542–2453.

Contact: Bob Spoerl, Program Specialist, New Hampshire Division of Parks and Recreation, Trails Bureau, P.O. Box 495, Concord, NH 03302-1856; (603) 271–2629.

• •

True to its name, the Sugar River Recreational Trail offers the unhurried traveler a sweet place to linger. This 10-mile trail hugs the river's wooded banks and crosses the river and its feeder stream on almost a dozen bridges. You'll encounter sturdy iron truss and girder bridges and small wooden ones, as well as the trail's two

A covered bridge along the Sugar River Recreational Trail.

masterpieces: a pair of covered bridges built by master woodworkers a century ago to carry trains from Newport to Claremont.

Like many railroads in New Hampshire, the Boston & Maine Railroad line from Concord to Claremont (completed in 1872) closed down in the 1960s after losing much of its business to highways. A small rail company bought the 10-mile stretch from Newport to Claremont and kept it running until 1977.

Traveling west out of Newport, the Sugar River Recreational Trail passes backyards and an open field before crossing the Sugar River at a small truss bridge. After crossing a road, the path parallels a cattle field, where shaggy Scotch Highland cattle may be grazing. The surface may be sandy in places; this is the softest part of the trail. If you look carefully into the woods on the right, you'll see three T-shaped stones and a 5-foot pillar. These are the remnants of a "rail rest," a structure once used for storing the extra rails needed to repair the track.

Two miles from Newport the Sugar River makes its northernmost bend and then widens as the river is joined by its northern branch. The river joins the Connecticut River a few miles west of Claremont.

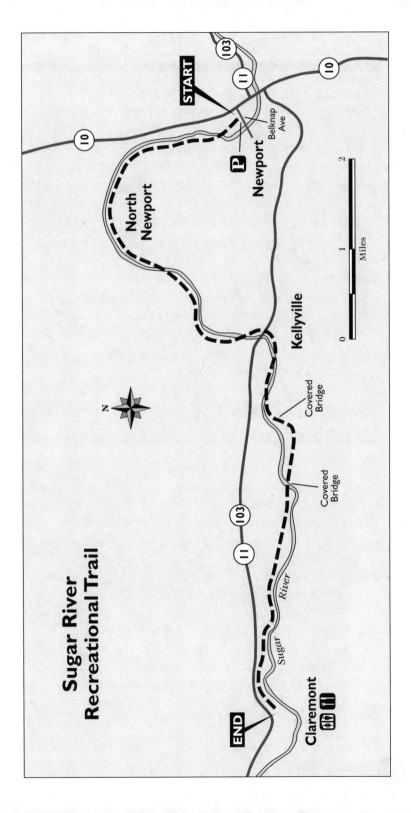

At this point the trail landscape becomes wooded with hemlock, pine, and a mix of hardwood trees surrounding the route. The river courses below in a ravine. In another half-mile the path reaches the first major bridge, an iron truss structure. After the first bridge, there is a second one. This bridge is made out of large iron plates, or girders, rather than trusses. These two bridges illustrate that when various engineers were involved in creating this railroad line, each one had his own specialty. Three more small bridges follow.

At the 5-mile mark (the trail's halfway point), you pass underneath the Route 11/103 bridge.

The first covered bridge appears a mile later. The covered bridges on the Sugar River Recreational Trail are two of just a handful of remaining covered rail bridges in the United States. An added benefit is that unlike most covered bridges in New England, this one has no motorized traffic on it. It's a good place to stop and relax. The handsome lattice work of this truss bridge wasn't built merely to be decorative. Its ingenious engineering design allowed the weight of a 100-ton-train to be shifted from truss to truss.

At about the 6.5-mile mark, a dirt road joins the rail-trail for about a quarter-mile before the path veers off again into the woods on the right. After another mile, the second covered bridge comes into view. It's slightly smaller—only about 130 feet long. Soon, the trail begins to parallel Route 11/103 on the right, eventually ending at an orange gate along the highway.

A half-mile or so farther along Route 103 is a large shopping center on the outskirts of Claremont. Continue into Claremont to view its classic New England architecture. You will also find a number of eateries.

Covered bridges are part of our nation's heritage.

MORE RAIL-TRAILS

Ⓚ Fremont Trail

An adjunct to the Rockingham Recreational Trail, the Fremont Trail offers an additional 6 miles of fun and adventure.

Activities:

Location: Rockingham County

Length: 6 miles

Surface: Dirt and gravel

Wheelchair access: No

Difficulty: Moderate

Food: There are restaurants in nearby Manchester, Epping, and Raymond.

Rest rooms: None

Seasons: Open year-round.

Access and parking: To get to the trail, take Route 101 to Route 125 north in Epping. Turn left on Route 125 north and continue for 0.5 mile until the road crosses Main Street. About 150 feet on the left is the start of the trail. The beginning of the Rockingham Trail is here, as well. Signs direct visitors to each trail.

Rentals:
- Bike Barn, Too, 14 East Broadway, Derry, NH; (603) 432–7907.
- Cycles Etceteras, 13 Range Road, Salem, NH; (603) 890–3212.
- Flying Wheels, 450 South Broadway, Salem, NH; (603) 893–0225.
- Merrimack Bicycle Shop, 1 Pinkerton Street, Derry, NH; (603) 437–0277.

Contact: Bob Spoerl, Program Specialist, New Hampshire Division of Parks and Recreation, Trails Bureau, P.O. Box 495, Concord, NH 03302-1856; (603) 271–2629.

The Nashua & Rochester Railroad built this line in 1874 as an extension of the Worcester & Nashua Railroad. The Boston & Maine Railroad bought it in 1886 and it became part of a line running between Worcester and Rochester. Passenger service ended in 1934.

The Fremont Trail is situated in the southeastern corner of New Hampshire. The 6-mile trail runs perpendicular to the Rockingham Trail and passes alongside a country road, through farmland and woods. Cows and horses can be seen grazing in nearby pastures, and even a hoof print or two along the path shows that the cows, too, have enjoyed strolling along the trail. The midsection of the trail offers the best ride for cyclists, with hard dirt and pretty scenery. At the 5-mile point the trail crosses an old railroad bridge. If you look down the brook to the right you can see an old dam that is now part of a privately owned farm. The trail ends after crossing the Exeter River Bridge. The last mile of the trail is quite sandy.

L Hillsborough Trail

The Hillsborough Trail offers a pleasant tour past farms and mills.

Activities:

Location: Hillsborough County

Length: 8.3 miles

Surface: Dirt and gravel, sandy in spots

Wheelchair access: No

Difficulty: Moderate

Food: There are restaurants in Bennington.

Rest rooms: None

Seasons: Open year-round.

Access and parking: From I–495, take Route 3 north. Once you enter New Hampshire, continue on Route 3 for 11 miles, then take exit 7 for Route 101 A. Turn left onto Route 101 A. After 9 miles the road becomes Route 101. Stay on Route 101 for 8 miles, then turn right onto Route 31 and travel 16 miles, through the town of Bennington. Take a right onto Old Stagecoach Road. The trail begins on the left side of the street.

Rentals:
- Nikki's Adventures, Francestown Road, Greenfield, NH; (603) 547–9994.
- Spokes and Slopes, 7 School Street #D, Peterborough, NH; (603) 924–9961.

Contact: Bob Spoerl, Program Specialist, New Hampshire Division of Parks and Recreation, Trails Bureau, P.O. Box 495, Concord, NH 03302-1856; (603) 271–2629.

The Contoocook Valley Railroad opened in 1849 and like many of the lines in the area, it was passed back and forth among different railroad companies. In 1884, it was bought by the Boston & Lowell Railroad, which operated the line for three years before it became part of the Boston & Maine Railroad. Passenger service continued on this line until 1936.

The 8.3-mile trail passes along a river, farmland, a small airport, and several mills. It is prettiest when it parallels the Contoocook River. The first half-mile of the trail can be discouraging, as the railroad tracks have not been removed. Cyclists can ride along to the right of the tracks. Once you've managed to get past the beginning of the trail, the path becomes a mix of dirt and gravel, although it can get sandy in places. Abandoned railroad cars alongside the trail give it a sense of history, as do the paper mills along the way. At 7.5 miles, the trail breaks for a bit. Follow Mill Street for about a quarter-mile, where the trail resumes on the left. At 8.3 miles, the trail ends at the remains of an old and crumbling mill, which blocks the trail.

Ⓜ Wolfeboro-Sanbornville Recreational Trail

This trail is still under development. It includes a park that highlights the area's railroad history.

Activities:

Location: Carroll County

Length: 12 miles

Surface: Crushed stone for the first 0.6 mile, making the trail suitable for bicycling only on that section. Rails are in place past the grade crossing of Routes 28 and 109. The trail is alongside the railroad tracks.

Wheelchair access: No

Difficulty: Moderate

Food: Restaurants are available in Wolfeboro and Sanborneville.

Rest rooms: None

Seasons: Open year-round.

Access and parking: From I-93 at the New Hampshire border, travel 23 miles to the exit for Route 3. Take a right. Go 3 miles until the road leads into Route 28. Continue on Route 28 for 49 miles until you reach the center of the town of Wolfeboro. The trail begins at the old passenger station.

Rentals: Nordic Skier, Main Street, Wolfeboro, NH; (603) 569–3151.

Contact: Bob Spoerl, Program Specialist, New Hampshire Division of Parks and Recreation, Trails Bureau, P.O. Box 495, Concord, NH 03302-1856; (603) 271–2629.

· ·

The Eastern Railroad built this line in 1872, when Wolfeboro was a thriving resort community. The line was bought by the Boston & Maine in 1892 and Wolfeboro became the rail line's division headquarters. A fire in the engine house in 1911 inspired Boston & Maine to move its operations to Dover. Passenger service was discontinued by 1936, and by the mid-1950s, freight service was greatly reduced. A last-ditch effort to retain the line was made in the early 1970s by Donald Hallock, who restored the depot and track and opened a passenger excursion trip on the former line. This venture, however, folded in 1986.

The Wolfeboro-Sanbornville Recreational Trail is a 12-mile rail-trail that features several lakes, a waterfall, and a nice park. Beginning at the restored Wolfeboro passenger station, the trail offers a nice blend of scenery. The first 0.6 mile has been improved with the addition of a packed-gravel surface and park benches along the path. This portion of the trail ends at the grade crossing of Routes 109 and 28. A 1,200-foot causeway allows you to traverse Crescent Lake. A longer causeway (1,800 feet long) provides access past Lake Wentworth. The path ends at the Sanbornville and Turntable Park, which has a memorial to the town's railroad past. This trail is being upgraded and may well be in improved condition in the next couple of years.

Ⓝ Zealand Recreation Area

The White Mountains are particularly beautiful and offer some excellent trails for adventurous souls. The mountains were once home to a network of railroads that served the region's lumber industry.

Activities:

Location: Grafton County

Length: Trails vary in length, elevation, and difficulty.

Surface: Packed dirt

Wheelchair access: Limited; rest rooms and campgrounds are accessible to wheelchairs.

Difficulty: Moderate

Food: There are several small convenience stores in Twin Mountain.

Rest rooms: In the campgrounds or at Zealand Picnic area (mid-May to Columbus Day).

Seasons: Open year-round. The campgrounds are open only from mid-May to Labor Day.

Access and parking: To get to the Zealand Valley trails, proceed 3 miles east of Twin Mountain on Route 302. Turn right onto Zealand Road to the entrance to the Zealand Recreation Area. The Sugarloaf Trail and Trestle Trail begin on the west side of the Zealand River Bridge. Proceed an additional 2.5 miles up Zealand Road to reach the parking lot for the Hale Brook Trail. The Zealand Trail is farther up the road, at 3.6 miles from the Route 302 turnoff. An annual parking pass costs $20. The weekly parking rate is $5.00 and the daily rate is $3.00. Permits can be bought at stores in Twin Mountains or at the ranger station.

Rentals:

- Joe Jones Ski and Sports, Route 45, Campton, NH; (603) 726–3000.
- Ski and Bike Warehouse, 112 Main Street, Lincoln, NH; (603) 745–3164.

Contact: White Mountain National Forest; (603) 869–2626.

- -

Lumber baron J. E. Henry was a man with a mission. In the late nineteenth century, he built a sawmill and railroad in the Zealand Valley to take advantage of the virgin timber there. By the turn of the twentieth century much of the original forest had been removed, and when several fires further devastated the forest, Henry's vision came to an end. The Zealand Valley has since been restored to its original beauty.

Henry's intricate railroad system is today smack dab in the middle of the White Mountain National Forest, and four of the rail corridors have been converted to recreational trails. The trails include the Sugarloaf Trail, the Hale Brook Trail, the Zealand Trail, and the Trestle Trail. The trails offer plenty of hiking adventures. Old second-growth forest surrounds the trails and there are mountain ponds, creeks, meadows, and swamplands nearby. Hike to the Mt. Hale summit at 4,054 feet elevation. Or climb Whitewall Mountain at 3,410 feet. Three Sugarloaf summits include the North Sugarloaf (2,310 feet), the Middle Sugarloaf (2,526 feet), and the South Sugarloaf (3,024 feet).

Future New Hampshire Rail-Trails

New Hampshire was once crisscrossed with short rail lines connecting forests and lumber mills. The many rail beds in the state now offer a wide variety of opportunities to build rail-trails, several of which are under development. The trails are in varied condition, with some trails slated to be completed in the near future, while others remain in very rough form. The best bet is to call the New Hampshire Trail Bureau to determine whether a particular rail-trail is in good enough shape for travel.

The 60-mile-long abandoned railroad right-of-way from Boscawen to Lebanon has been purchased by the State of New Hampshire and is currently administered by the New Hampshire Bureau of Trails. The railroad ties are still in place on the abandoned roadbed.

Several rail-trails are planned in and around Manchester. The Portsmouth Branch Rail-Trail will run to South Manchester. In West Manchester, an 8-mile trail will parallel the Piscatqug River to the edge of Glen Lake and into downtown Goffstown. Both trails will be joined using an abandoned railroad bridge across the Merrimack River.

A 6-mile rail-trail from Rindge-Jaffrey is being considered. It would run northward to Peterboro and possibly beyond. Several sections of the Cheshire County Rail-Trails are open but still need some work. These trails include 8.9 miles of an abandoned right-of-way within Hinsdale, an additional 21 miles from Hinsdale to Keene, and 42 miles between Fitzwilliam and Walpole.

A 9-mile rail-trail has been proposed to run between East Haverhill to Woodsville. An extension running from Woodsville to Littleton is also in the planning stage. The railroad bed has recently been abandoned and cleared of all rails and ties. Bridge work still needs to be completed before the trail can be opened to public use. This is true also of the abandoned right-of-way between Jefferson and Gorham.

The Lakes Region Connector Trail is a proposed trail that would pass through the towns of Franklin, Northfield, Tilton, Sanbornton, Belmont, Gilford, Laconia, Meredith, Center Harbor, and Moultonborough.

Twenty-six rail-trails in the White Mountain National Forest range in length from 1 to 11 miles. The trails are administered by the White Mountain National Forest. These trails are primarily maintained as hiking trails. The Appalachian Mountain Club (AMC) has spent considerable time and energy cataloging these trails. Their offices, located in Beacon Hill in Boston, provide the best information on the trails in the White Mountains. Call the AMC at (617) 523–0636 or the ranger station at the White Mountain National Forest at (603) 528–8721.

Rails-to-Trails

RHODE ISLAND

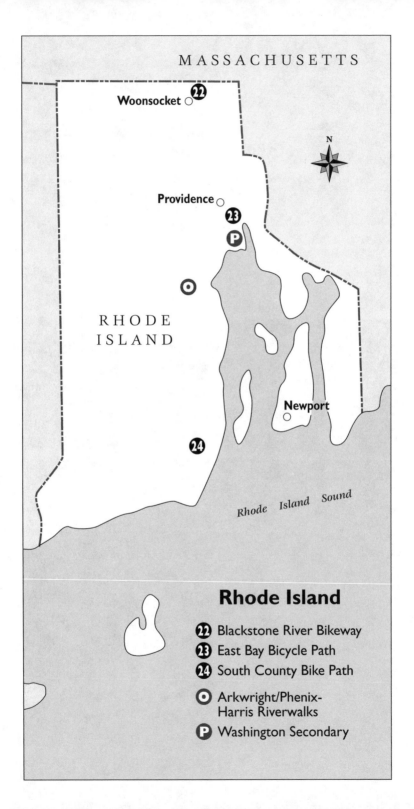

MASSACHUSETTS

Woonsocket ○ 🄮

N

Providence ○

🄯

🅟

◉

RHODE
ISLAND

Newport
○

🄰

Rhode Island Sound

Rhode Island

🄮 Blackstone River Bikeway
🄯 East Bay Bicycle Path
🄰 South County Bike Path

◉ Arkwright/Phenix-
Harris Riverwalks
🅟 Washington Secondary

INTRODUCTION

Rhode Island, the smallest state in the nation, is only 48 miles long and 37 miles wide, but within its borders are 400 miles of shoreline and a surprisingly diverse landscape. Founded in 1636 by religious dissenters from the Massachusetts Bay Colony, and later playing a key political role in the American Revolution, Rhode Island retains today a tradition of autonomy and independent ways.

Its capital and largest city, Providence, is undergoing considerable renovation and renewal. Be sure to visit Benefit Street, where more than 200 restored buildings are located. Here you will find an assortment of eighteenth- and nineteenth-century homes, schools, taverns, and shops built by sea captains and shipbuilders.

Newport has long been a favorite haunt of the rich and famous. The mansions lining Bellevue Avenue and Ocean Drive have been the summertime homes of many of our nation's best known families. It was here that President John F. Kennedy and Jacqueline Kennedy were married at St. Mary's Church.

Rhode Island's rail-trails include the East Bay Rail-Trail, which begins near Providence and follows Narragansett Bay to the pretty seaside town of Bristol. Eastern Rhode Island boasts the South County Bikeway, which opened in 1999 and is in wonderful condition. In northern Rhode Island the Blackstone River Bikeway is particularly pretty. Seven more rail-trails are projected for Rhode Island, covering 78 miles.

Rhode Island's

TOP RAIL-TRAILS

22 Blackstone River Bikeway

Located in the northernmost tip of Rhode Island, this is a gem of a rail-trail, scenic from start to finish.

Activities:

Location: Providence County

Length: 3.5 miles

Surface: Asphalt

Wheelchair access: Yes

Difficulty: Easy

Food: Various eateries are available in Lincoln.

Rest rooms: Lincoln Woods State Park

Seasons: Open year-round.

Access and parking: From I–95 north, take Route 146 and proceed north for about 10 minutes. Take a right onto Break Neck Hill Road. The road winds around a bit before entering a commercial business area. Go past the shopping center for about 0.5 mile, then take a left into Blackstone State Park.

Rentals:

- B + B Cycle and Sports, 149 Reservoir Road, Lincoln, RI; (401) 725–2830.
- AA Vittorio Cycle, 538 Wood Avenue, Woonsocket, RI; (401) 765–3275.

Contact: Lisa Lawless, Rhode Island Department of Environmental Management, 83 Park Street, Providence, RI 02903-1037; (401) 222–6800.

The Blackstone River Bikeway is part of the National Heritage Corridor, which celebrates the birthplace of the American Revolution. In nearby Pawtucket, America's first water-powered cotton-

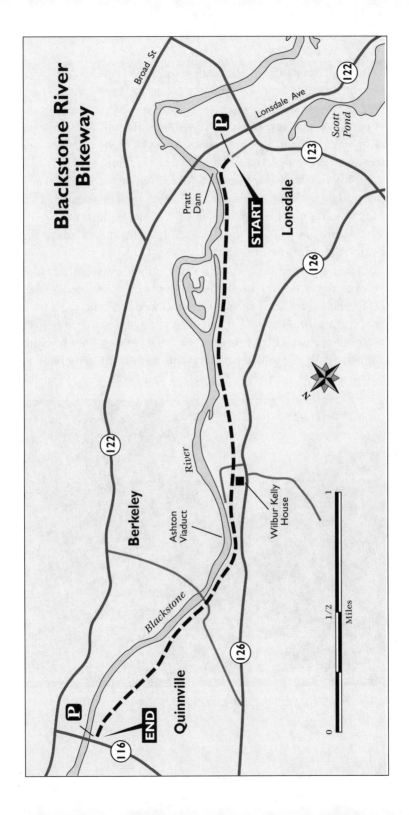

spinning mill opened in 1790, precipitating the rapid industrialization of the area. By the mid-eighteenth century, Providence, Rhode Island, and Worcester, Massachusetts, were two of the largest manufacturing cities in New England. In 1828 a canal was built between the two cities to help transport goods. In 1847 the Providence and Worcester Railroad opened a line following the same route.

After leaving the parking lot, pay close attention to the sign, which directs you the right way onto the trail. Don't pick up speed just yet as there is an interesting sight on the right of the trail from the parking lot, where you will find the stone abutment remains from a former railroad bridge over the Pratt Dam.

For the next mile, there is water on both sides of the corridor. The elevated trail is quite pretty here, lined with open wood fences. At 1.3 miles, the trail crosses over a small wooden bridge. There is a slight incline onto the bridge, so proceed slowly. At 1.7 miles, the path crosses a road with a bridge on the right. Watch for oncoming traffic. The path continues to follow the river until it veers away from the water at 2.2 miles. Just when you think you are in the

Open wood fences line the Blackstone River Bikeway.

middle of rural Rhode Island, the daunting remains of a factory appear on the other side of the river at 2.4 miles. The factory is now only 5 percent occupied. The juxtaposition of the rural and industrial defines this area, where much of the Industrial Revolution began in the United States. It was here that the first American industrialists determined that it was

Remains of an old factory that once thrived along the Blackstone River when Providence was one of the largest manufacturing cities in New England.

possible to harness the water to provide power for factories.

Also take note of the Wilbur Kelly House, on the left. This former gatekeeper's home will be the site of the Blackstone River Valley National Heritage Museum, now in the planning stage.

At 2.6 miles, the trail passes under the Ashton Viaduct Bridge restoration site. Also of historical significance, the Ashton Viaduct was built in the 1930s. The wonderful arches are being restored to their original glory. Bridges like this one were built at a time when labor was cheap but materials were expensive. The designers of the bridges went to great trouble to minimize the cost of the supplies. Slow down and follow the directions of the workmen in the area.

After passing the construction site, the path becomes more heavily forested but begins a steady incline. This is a good place to turn around for less hearty souls. The trail continues for about another mile until it ends at a parking lot.

The trail offers the best way to get to the beach from downtown Providence and is well worth a visit.

Activities:

Location: Greater Providence and Bristol Counties

Length: 14.5 miles

Surface: Asphalt

Wheelchair access: Yes

Difficulty: Easy

Food: There are many restaurants in Warren and Bristol.

Rest rooms: During the summer months, there are several rest room facilities open in Colt Park and one in Haines Park. Porta-johns are placed adjacent to the trail during the winter months.

Seasons: Open year-round.

Access and parking: From I–95, take Route 44 to Riverside (the first exit on the east side of the Washington Bridge). A small parking lot is to the right and lies immediately adjacent to the trail. A map and information booth are located next to the parking lot.

Rentals:
- Bay Path Cycle, 13 State Street, Bristol, RI; (401) 254–1277.
- Your Bike Shop, 51 Cole Street, Warren, RI; (401) 254–9755.

Transportation: Contact the Rhode Island Public Transit Authority; (401) 781–9400.

Contact: Kevin O'Malley, Regional Manager, Colt State Park, Bristol, RI 02809; (401) 253–7482; fax (401) 253–6766.

. . . .

The corridor was originally developed by the Providence and Worcester Railroad. The stretch of line that is now the East Bay Bicycle Path was used to ferry passengers between Providence and the quiet resort towns along Narragansett Bay. The corridor was abandoned in the late 1970s and the East Bay Bicycle Path was

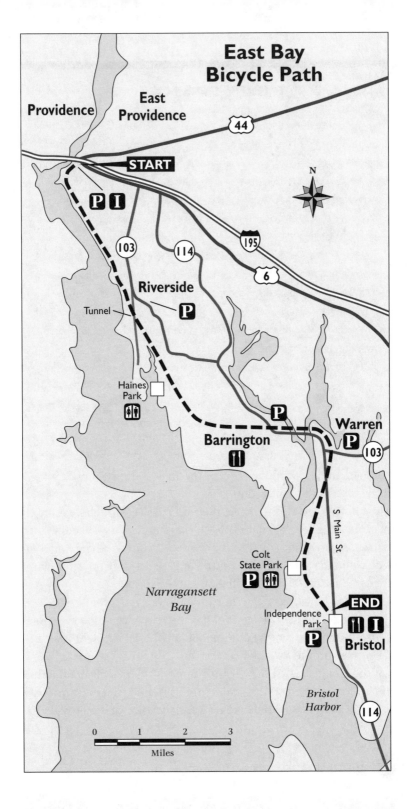

East Bay
Bicycle Path

Providence

East
Providence

44

N

START

P I

195

103

114

6

Riverside

P

Tunnel

Haines
Park

P

P

Warren

P 103

Barrington

S Main St

Colt
State Park

P

Independence
Park

P

END

Bristol

Narragansett
Bay

Bristol
Harbor

114

0   1   2   3

Miles

PROVIDENCE

The city of Providence has been getting a considerable amount of attention lately. It even has a television series named after it. And well it should. Founded in 1636 by Roger Williams, who was thrown out of Massachusetts for his religious beliefs, he named the city "for God's merciful providence unto me in my distress." Initially a shipping and ship-building town, Providence sent ships to such faraway places as the East and West Indies, Africa, and China.

Take some time to walk along Benefit Street, where the restoration of nineteenth-century mansions and shops will give you a chance to see how the city must have looked in its glorious seafaring days.

Providence has experienced considerable urban renewal, as evidenced by the beautiful Providence Place Mall, home to a number of department stores, restaurants, and cinemas.

Providence is the capital of the state and is also home to prestigious Brown University and the Rhode Island School of Design. For more information about the city, call the Greater Providence Convention and Visitors Bureau at (401) 751–1177 or (800) 233–1636 (outside of Rhode Island).

developed and built in five stages—the first section opened in 1987 and the last section opened in 1993.

Just before the 1-mile mark, the trail passes through East Providence. Heading south toward Bristol, water and boats will come into view—mostly on the right, but there are a few areas where small inlets or wetlands abut the trail on the left. In warmer months, clammers can be seen digging in shallows along the route.

Near the 1-mile mark, the trail parallels Veteran's Memorial Highway. A wooden fence runs part of the way down the road to protect trail users from the nearby automobile traffic. To the right is an unblocked view of the Providence skyline.

At the 2-mile mark, the trail encounters a steep grade. As the trail veers to the right, a very steep downhill should be taken cautiously by cyclists. Water surrounds the trail and the view of the Providence

skyline again comes into view. Old railroad tracks can be seen running alongside the trail here before the trail crosses a small bridge.

Before the 3-mile mark, the trail is surrounded by cliffs and water, providing homes for pelicans, egrets, swans, geese—and the occasional turtle. The area around the trail becomes more suburban and less industrial. Just before mile 4, the trail passes through a tunnel under Bullocks Point Avenue leading to the town of Riverside. Take a break here at the nearby ice-cream shop. Or take a one-half-mile detour to the Looff Carousel in Crescent Park. The carousel was built in 1895 and features sixty-six hand-carved horses. The carousel is open during the summer months.

After crossing Turner Avenue in Riverside, the trail widens a bit and there are more shady areas along the route. Nearing the 5-mile mark, the trail begins to feel more secluded with the surrounding forests providing a nice buffer from nearby civilization.

At mile 6, the trail reaches Haines Park, a perfect place for a picnic. At mile 8, wildflowers line the trail throughout the summer and their sweet smell fills the air. Soon the forest opens up again providing spectacular views of Narragansett Bay.

Shortly thereafter, the trail runs through the quiet town of Barrington. Take a break at one of the several eateries along the way. After crossing the main road in Barrington (County Road), an old stone wall and culvert run along the right side of the path. While entering the town of Warren the trail crosses two wooden bridges, with more great views of the water. Between the two bridges is an old brick American Tourister factory on the right. On the left is a beautiful wetlands area with tall cattails,

Enterprising children sell refreshments along the trail in the summer.

where clammers can be spotted trying their luck.

Past the 10-mile mark, the trail enters downtown Warren. A number of eateries are available, as are bicycle and in-line skating rentals.

Another breathtaking view of Narragansett Bay comes into view at mile marker 11. The trail then passes through a wetland area where cattails tower over you, forming a natural tunnel. The trail then begins a gradual, mile-long ascent, starting around the 11.5-mile point.

By mile 13, the trail levels out again and small houses line both sides of the trail. At Asylum Road, you can turn right into Colt State Park, where rest rooms, picnic tables, and waterfront views are available. Boat-launching facilities also are found here. From Colt State Park, you can reach Bristol Town Beach, which is the best place along the route to do a little sunbathing.

At the 14-mile marker, the trail approaches the town of Bristol. The trail skirts within a few feet of Narragansett Bay on the right, with boats dotting the horizon. Several seafood restaurants on the left welcome trailblazers to stop and try some of Rhode Island's famous clams and lobsters.

The East Bay Bicycle Path ends at Independence Park in Bristol, where more trail parking and another map and information booth can be found. The park, which was dedicated to Bristol Navy veterans, offers grassy areas and a short boardwalk from which to admire the view.

In-line skaters enjoy the path.

The South County Bike Path offers a pleasant ride through a mix of rural and suburban landscapes.

Activities:

Location: Kingston

Length: 4.3 miles

Surface: Asphalt

Wheelchair access: Yes

Difficulty: Easy

Food: Eateries are available in nearby Kingston.

Rest rooms: Kingston Railroad Station

Seasons: Open year-round.

Access and parking: From Providence, take I–95 south to Route 4 south (exit 9). Take a left at the end of the exit and travel on Route 4 for 14 miles until you reach Route 138. Take a right and continue for about 6 miles, past the University of Rhode Island. About 1 mile past the university is the Kingston train station, where parking is available. The trailhead is just above the parking lot, to the left, and is well marked.

Rentals: Ron's Bicycle Shop, 7592 Post Road, North Kingstown, RI; (401) 294–2238.

Contact: Steve Devine, Supervising Planner, Rhode Island Department of Transportation, Two Capitol Hill, Providence, RI 02903; (401) 222–2023, extension 4063.

• •

T his short rail-trail opened recently and is the pride of the community. Already a favorite among the locals, it offers a pleasant experience to anyone visiting the area.

The Narragansett Pier Railroad was built in 1876 and primarily served the purpose of transporting tourists to Narragansett Pier, where the line met ferry boats to the islands in Narragansett Bay. After World War II, a portion of the line was abandoned (from Narragansett Pier to Peacedale), and regular passenger service was discontinued. Freight

Learning how to ride a bicycle along the South County Bike Path.

service continued into the 1970s. In 1982, the Town of South Kingstown acquired the portion of right-of-way between the Saugatucket River and the intersection of Charles and Robinson Streets.

The trail begins just north of the railroad station. Do not pick up speed right away as you will need to make a stop at the Liberty Lane road crossing, about 150 feet from the beginning of the trail. Initially, the path travels past light industry on both sides of the trail. At .9 mile, the path crosses a small bridge over the Chipuret River. The trail becomes more rural at this point, and at 1.5 miles the path crosses a second bridge, this one over White Horn Brook. It is quite pretty here with water on both sides of the trail and views of marshlands.

At 1.8 miles, the path begins a steady incline for the next 0.2 mile. At 2.1 miles, an open wooden fence begins to line the trail. At 2.3 miles, the path travels past Tefft Hill on the left, a lovely, wooded, hilly area. Use caution at the South Road crossing at 3.0 miles. The path becomes more suburban here, with houses on both sides. At 3.4 miles, the trail passes Kingstown Athletic Field, which comprises an assortment of sport fields. At 3.7 miles is another road crossing at Kingston Road. Again, use caution as automobiles travel quickly on these back roads. Once on the other side of Kingston Road, the path is lined by a rock embankment on the right shoulder. The path ends at 4.3 miles. There are plans to extend the rail-trail to Narragansett Pier.

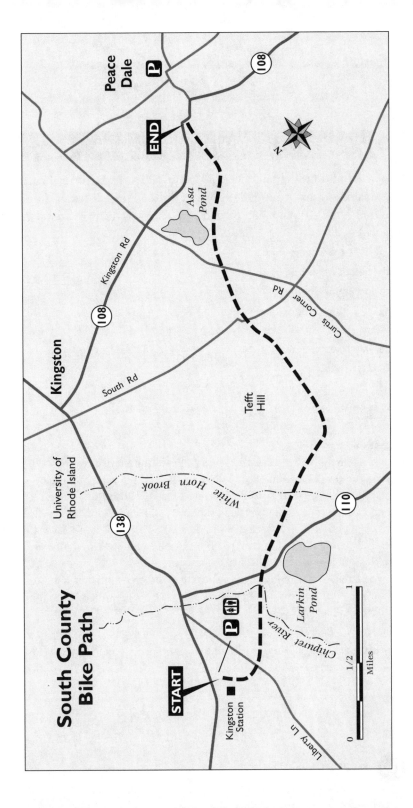

MORE RAIL-TRAILS

◎ Arkwright/Phenix-Harris Riverwalks

The residents of the small towns of Phenix-Harris and Arkwright are interested in transforming their former railroad lines into rail-trails. The trails are still rough but are good for a short walk away from the highway.

Activities:

Location: Kent County

Length: 2 miles (approximately 1 mile each)

Surface: Dirt

Wheelchair access: Yes

Difficulty: Easy

Food: There are restaurants in the towns of Arkwright and Phenix-Harris.

Rest rooms: None

Seasons: Open year-round.

Access and parking:

- *To reach the Phenix Riverwalk:* From I–95 southbound, take the I–295 north/Route 113 exit and bear left at the fork in the ramp. Merge onto East Avenue (Route 113). Turn left onto Bald Hill Road (Route 2 south), then turn left onto Toll Gate Road (Route 115). Follow Route 115, which twists slightly left and becomes Providence Street and then East Main Street. Turn left off of Route 115 onto Lincoln Avenue. The trailhead is on the left, about a half-block up the street.

- *To reach the Arkwright Riverwalk:* return to Main Street and turn left. Continue on Main 1 mile to the Arkwright Mills. The Riverwalk is behind the mills on the left.

Rentals: Joe's Bike Shop, 661 Oaklawn Avenue, Cranston, RI; (401) 275-0800.

Contact: Jack McGillivray, Pawtuxet River Authority; (401) 739-7635.

These short riverwalks are tucked away and run parallel to Route 115. The Phenix-Harris Riverwalk lies directly behind the downtown area and is quite shaded for the short distance of the trail. A small river separates the walk from downtown. The Arkwright Riverwalk is directly behind the Arkwright Mills. The 1-mile walk parallels the river. Efforts by the Pawtuxet River Authority are now underway to improve both trails.

(P) Washington Secondary

Much of Cranston is commercial, with long stretches of light industry lining its streets, which is why the Washington Secondary rail-trail is a special place. It offers a quiet alternative to city living. With the possibility of the trail being extended into Connecticut, the rail-trail will bring further enjoyment to its travelers.

Activities:

Location: Cranston

Length: 4.5 miles

Surface: Asphalt

Wheelchair access: Yes

Difficulty: Easy

Food: Cranston has a variety of restaurants and convenience stores.

Rest rooms: None

Seasons: Open year-round.

Access and parking: From Providence, take I–95 South to Route 2 (Reservoir Avenue). At the third light, take a right onto Route 12. At the first light, take a right onto Ganset Avenue. Park at the Hugh B. Bain Middle School parking lot. The trail is northwest of the parking lot on the other side of the soccer field and track.

Rentals: Joe's Bike Shop, 661 Oaklawn Avenue, Cranston, RI; (401) 275-0800.

Contact: Steve Devine, Supervising Planner, State of Rhode Island; (401) 222–2023, extension 4063.

· ·

The Washington Secondary Track was built in the 1840s by the Hartford, Providence, and Fishkill Railroad. Once called the Rhode Island

Railroad, the rail line was primarily used to transport freight to manufacturers and lumber yards.

The portion of the rail-trail recently opened is a state-of-the-art path with an asphalt surface. The trail is particularly popular with families and children. Tucked away in the working-class neighborhood of Cranston, this 4.5-mile rail-trail offers a pleasant ride through light forest. The trail initially passes through an industrial area before it becomes more secluded. The path is then quite pretty for a couple miles, with trees lining both sides of the trail. For the last mile, the trail parallels a major road with plenty of small businesses along the way, including several food stands. Plans are to extend this trail for an additional 20 miles and to connect it to the Trestle Trail at the Connecticut state line.

Future New Hampshire Rail-Trails

Rhode Island has a vision to connect several trails so that eventually there will be a trail leading directly from Providence into Connecticut. The plan calls for the extension of the Washington Secondary Rail-Trail to the Trestle Trail, which would in turn connect with the Moosup-Sterling Trail in Connecticut.

Other plans include the North-West Bike Path, which is currently under design and would be part of the Woonasquatec River Greenway. The plan would allow for a rail-trail to be built connecting Providence to Scituate. In the more southern part of the state, plans call for expanding the South County Bike Path another 4 miles.

Rails-to-Trails

VERMONT

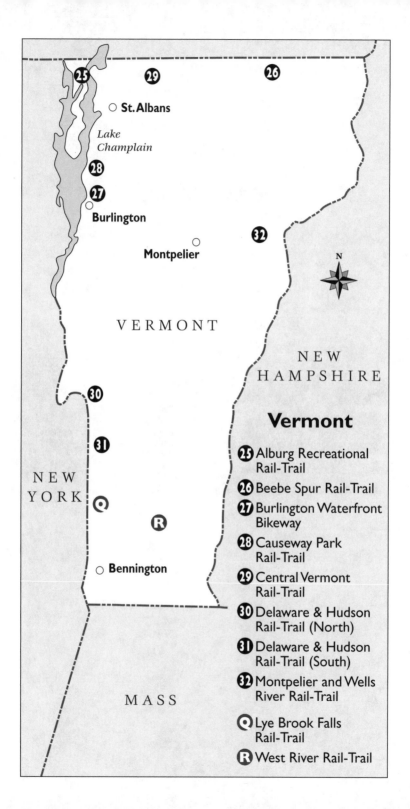

St. Albans

Lake Champlain

Burlington

Montpelier

VERMONT

NEW HAMPSHIRE

NEW YORK

Bennington

MASS

N

Vermont

25 Alburg Recreational Rail-Trail

26 Beebe Spur Rail-Trail

27 Burlington Waterfront Bikeway

28 Causeway Park Rail-Trail

29 Central Vermont Rail-Trail

30 Delaware & Hudson Rail-Trail (North)

31 Delaware & Hudson Rail-Trail (South)

32 Montpelier and Wells River Rail-Trail

Q Lye Brook Falls Rail-Trail

R West River Rail-Trail

INTRODUCTION

V ermont's beauty cannot be surpassed. Be prepared to ooh and aah your way through the state. The northern part, often referred to as the Upper Valley, is unspoiled. Here you will find farmlands and dairy farms. The back roads take you through small towns that are postcard perfect. Spend some time in Woodstock, which was established in the 1790s. The town has often been ranked as one of the top ten prettiest towns in the country. Woodstock's well-preserved homes and village green bespeak old New England charm.

Burlington, Vermont's largest city, is located on Lake Champlain. Settled in 1775, the city's oldest section is found along Battery, Pearl, South William, and Church Streets. Be sure to visit the Church Street Marketplace, a 4-block pedestrian mall located in the historic district.

But it is Vermont's 370,000-acre Green Mountain National Forest that defines the state. With more than 500 miles of trails, including the Appalachian/Long Trail, there are endless outdoor activities. Several popular ski areas are located in the Green Mountains, including Stowe, Mount Snow, Burke Mountain, and Sugarbush.

Vermont's rail-trails are equally exquisite. The Causeway Rail-Trail, just north of Burlington, is especially noteworthy: The original line was built to connect Vermont to Canada, atop a causeway constructed primarily of marble slabs. Nearby, the Burlington Waterfront Rail-Trail also offers splendid views of the lake.

In Western Vermont the two Delaware and Hudson Rail-Trails take you through unspoiled regions with plenty of lakes and ponds and forest to keep your senses busy. The Beebe Spur Rail-Trail at the northern tip of the state follows Lake Memphremagog to the Canadian border.

With twelve established rail-trails in the state covering 134 miles, there are plenty of opportunities to get to know the state better. An additional eleven rail-trails are in the development stages.

Vermont's

• • • • • • • • • • • • • • • • • •

TOP RAIL-TRAILS

25 Alburg Recreational Rail-Trail

A short but superb trail nestled in the remote, lake-filled region of northwestern Vermont—just a few miles from the Canadian border. Several wildlife refuges are nearby.

Activities:

Location: Grand Isle County

Length: 3.5 miles

Surface: Hard-packed cinder and gravel

Wheelchair access: Limited

Difficulty: Easy

Food: Restaurants and food stores are available in Alburg.

Rest rooms: None

Seasons: Open year-round.

Access and parking: From State Route 78, take Route 2 north 2 miles into Alburg. The municipal building is on the left. Directly across from the Alburg Fire Station, turn right onto Industrial Park Drive. The road ends in a circle that was once occupied by a railroad roundhouse. The trail begins to the left of the circle's center. You can park around the circle, and there is also plenty of street parking in Alburg.

Rentals:

- Earl's Cycling & Fitness, 135 Main Street, Burlington, VT; (802) 862–4203.
- Vermont's Outdoor Sports Headquarters, 85 Main Street, Burlington, VT; (802) 658–3313.
- North Star Cyclery,100 Main Street, Burlington, VT; (802) 863–3832.

Contact: Charles Vile, Forestry District Manager, Vermont Department of Environmental Protection, 111 West Street, Essex Junction, VT 05452-4615; (802) 879–6565; fax (802) 879–3871; cvile@anressex.ant.state.vt.us.

• • • • • • • • • • • • • • • • • • • •

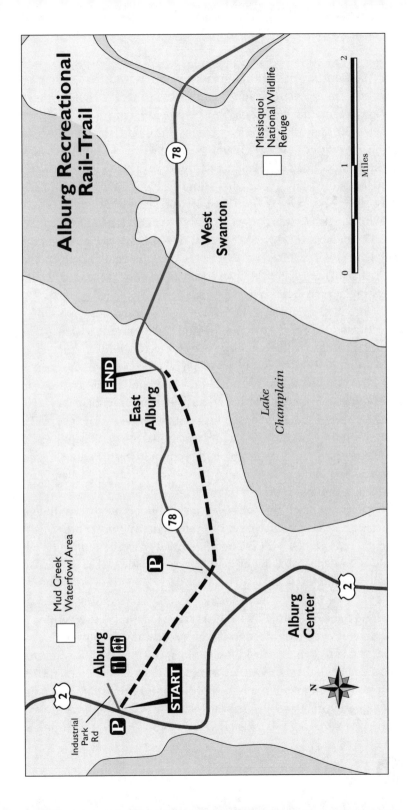

The Central Vermont Railroad was one of two railroad companies in a race to reach Burlington in the 1840s. They both reached Vermont's largest city by 1849 before continuing north to Alburg. The Central Vermont corridor continued north of Burlington on the east side of Lake Champlain all the way to Montreal, while the Rutland Railroad took a significantly more difficult route between the islands of Lake Champlain. Rutland abandoned its line in the early 1960s and Central Vermont followed suit soon thereafter.

While the trail starts out with a gravely ballast, it turns to a harder-pack cinder fairly quickly. Take note of the wetlands to the right of the trail, where you are likely to see at least one great blue heron. To the left are farmlands that yield to an expansive field of goldenrod, which gives way in turn to a marshy wetland.

Before the 1-mile mark, the vista to the left will unfold into a magnificent wetland area known as the Mud Creek Waterfowl Area. This wildlife preserve is home to dozens of species of birds.

Within 1.5 miles, the trail crosses a small, rustic wooden bridge that offers a view to the wetlands on either side of the trail. From here, Route 78, which marks the eastern edge of the wildlife preserve, is visible. This is a busy road, so use caution when crossing at grade.

From here, the trail gets progressively narrower as it passes by woods on either side. At 2.4 miles, the trail crosses Blue Rock Road at grade. You can catch some wonderful views of Lake Champlain by turning right onto the paved road.

Back on the trail, the path remains shrouded in trees, although there is an occasional farm on the right side. Within another half-mile, the path crosses a private gravel road that leads into a development known as McGregor Point. The trail passes a set of railroad tracks before ending abruptly at Route 78.

If you look closely, you will notice a Y in the remaining tracks. At one time three different railroad lines came together at this point and locomotives changed direction before proceeding over Lake Champlain or heading into Canada. The bridge over Lake Champlain has long since been dismantled, but you can cross the lake on Route 78.

If you haven't seen enough wildlife, cross the bridge and continue another mile to the Missisquoi National Wildlife Refuge. Covering nearly 6,000 acres, this refuge is a haven for waterfowl and mammals.

26 Beebe Spur Rail-Trail

The Beebe Spur Rail-Trail opened in 1999. It parallels Lake Memphremagog and takes its guests through some beautiful Vermont woods.

Activities:

Location: Orleans County

Length: 4.0 miles

Surface: Packed gravel

Wheelchair access: Yes

Difficulty: Easy

Food: There are numerous food establishments in Newport.

Rest rooms: None

Seasons: Open year-round.

Access and parking: Take Route 9 north to Route 28 east. When you reach the intersection of Routes 28 and 5, take a right onto Route 5 north (also known as Shattuck Hill Road), which will turn into North Derby Road. At Prouty Drive, take a left. The trail will be on the right. Parking is limited, so the best bet is to proceed about 0.25 mile past the trail entrance and park in the hospital parking lot.

Rentals: None

Contact: Amy Bell, Bicycle and Pedestrian Coordinator, Local Transportation Facilities, State of Vermont Agency of Transportation, 133 State Street, Montpelier, VT 05633; (802) 828–5799; amy.bell@state.vt.us.

• •

The special charm of this trail is the ease with which you can travel amid forest and lake views, with the final thrill of reaching the Canadian border. This is Vermont at its best.

Once a spur line for the Canadian Pacific, the railroad transported freight (primarily lumber and grain) from Sherbrook, Quebec, to Wells Rivers in Vermont. Passenger service was also available until the 1960s. Originally part of the Boston & Maine Railroad and built in the late 1800s, the line was eventually bought by the Canadian

Beautiful Lake Memphremagog extends 8 miles into the United States and another 20 miles into Canada.

Pacific. After service was discontinued, the State of Vermont began the process of trail conversion in 1996.

The beginning of the trail is wide with trees lining both sides. The backyards of summer homes can be seen on the right. At 0.8 mile, a newly constructed wooden bridge takes you past meadows on both sides. Lake Memphremagog (the lake's name is derived from an Indian word meaning "beautiful lake") is on the left and the mountains can be seen in the distance. The lake extends 8 miles into the United States and an additional 20 miles into Canada.

At 1.2 miles, the path crosses at Orrwood and Lindsey Road, with the lake continuing to the left of the trail. The next mile offers pleasant views of lakes, woods, and occasional vacation homes. At 2.3 miles, the trail crosses a second bridge, with the lake still dominating the landscape on the left.

At 3.3 miles a third bridge is crossed as the trail opens up to marshlands on both sides of the path. At 3.4 miles, the trail crosses a road at grade. Use caution. The U.S. portion of the trail ends at 4.0 miles, where a sign is posted to indicate that you have reached the Canadian border.

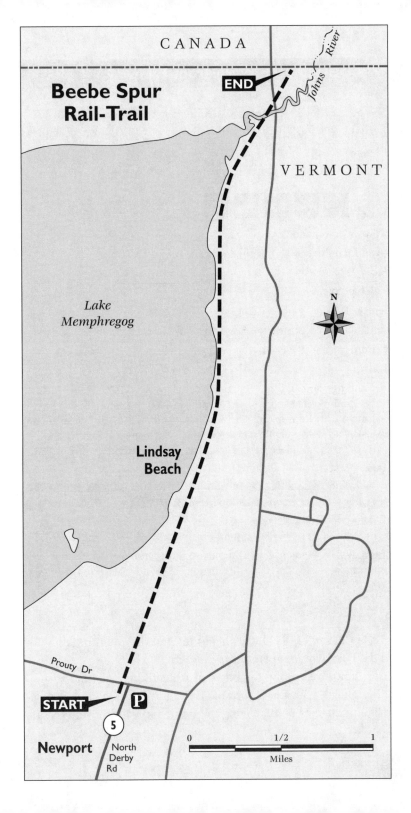

CANADA

**Beebe Spur
Rail-Trail**

END

Johns River

VERMONT

*Lake
Memphregog*

N

**Lindsay
Beach**

Prouty Dr

START

P

5

Newport

North
Derby
Rd

0   1/2   1

Miles

The best of Lake Champlain's waterfront can be experienced on this bikeway. There are outdoor opportunities for people of all ages.

Activities:

Location: Chittenden County

Length: 7.5 miles

Surface: Asphalt

Wheelchair access: Yes

Difficulty: Easy

Food: The town of Burlington has a wide range of restaurants.

Rest rooms: Oakridge Park

Seasons: Open year-round.

Access and parking: From I–189, take Shelburne Road (U.S. Route 7). Turn left onto Flynn Avenue and proceed 0.8 mile to Oakledge Park, located on the waterfront of Lake Champlain. The park has rest rooms, a bath house, tennis courts, baseball fields, picnic tables, shelters, and a small beach with a lifeguard. It is a pleasant place to start your trip on the Burlington Bikeway.

Rentals:

- Earl's Cycling & Fitness, 135 Main Street, Burlington, VT; (802) 862–4203.
- Vermont's Outdoor Sports Headquarters, 85 Main Street, Burlington, VT; (802) 658–3313.
- North Star Cyclery,100 Main Street, Burlington, VT; (802) 863–3832.

Contact: Robert Whalen, Superintendent, Burlington Department of Park and Recreation, 1 La Valley Lane, Burlington, VT 05401-2779; (802) 865–7247; fax (802) 865–7247.

• •

Lake Champlain is always beautiful and the rail-trail is one of the best ways to spend time close to the shore.

The Central Vermont Railroad constructed this line (and several parallel routes), with the first train arriving in Burlington in December 1849. Industry boomed along the route and within twenty years

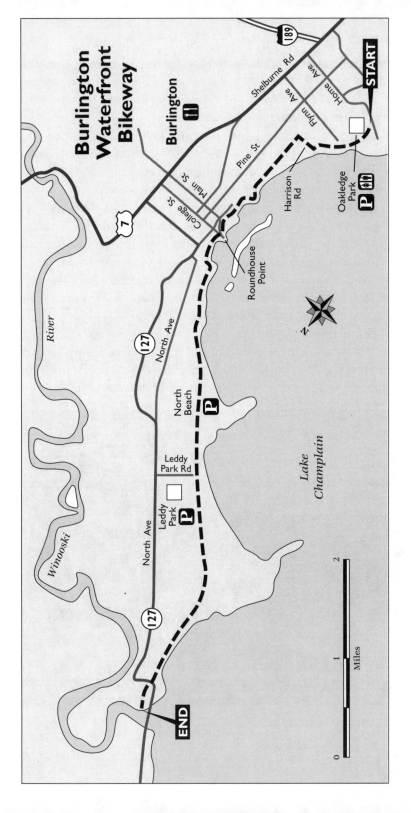

Burlington had become the nation's third-largest lumber port (behind Chicago and Albany). Although the lumber business went into a decline before the turn of the century, the railroad route continued to thrive well into the twentieth century.

The city acquired the line in the early 1970s and developed it in sections, completing the entire trail by 1987. Central Vermont's mainline, which links the Canadian and U.S. rail systems, still exists and parallels the trail's southern section.

Head right out of the parking lot to get to the start of the trail. As you start on the path, the shores of Lake Champlain line the left side. At 0.3 mile, the path veers from the lake temporarily. To get to the actual rail corridor, turn right onto Harrison Avenue and travel three short blocks to the railroad tracks. Take a left here, where the trail parallels an existing set of tracks for 1 mile and cuts through a light industrial area that ends at Roundhouse Point.

There are several benches, a picnic area, rest rooms, and a boat launch between Roundhouse Point and Perkins Piers. Sculptures and attractive plantings line the waterfront along this section of the trail. Stop at one of the many benches to enjoy the dramatic views.

Lake Champlain lines one side of the rail-trail.

The trail continues off to the right and weaves through a large parking lot as it skirts downtown Burlington. Several restaurants and shops are located here, and you can venture into the pedestrian-friendly city via King Street, Main Street, or College Street.

Back on the trail, the path continues to parallel a set of railroad tracks before entering Waterfront Park and Promenade. This well-manicured green space was a joint project of Burlington citizens, the State of Vermont, and the Central Vermont Railroad. At this end of the park, which offers public phones and water fountains, you can catch a shuttle bus into town, using a bus equipped with bike racks.

Beyond Waterfront Park, the active rail lines veer away from the trail and the 40-acre Burlington Urban Reserve lines the left side. In less than a mile, the trail heads uphill, until you arrive atop a high ridge that provides sweeping views of the city, Lake Champlain, and the Adirondack Mountains in New York.

At about 3.5. miles, the trail cuts through an area called North Beach, where a campground, picnic area, playgrounds, parking, a bathhouse, and a beach are available. This marks the trail's midpoint and offers a wonderful spot to enjoy a picnic or a swim.

The next mile of trail is pleasantly wooded with maple, oak, sumac, and willow trees, creating the green setting. The trail passes through a residential area before reaching Leddy Park at the 4.5-mile mark. Here you will find abundant parking, as well as softball diamonds, soccer fields, tennis and basketball courts, and rest rooms. You can swim or sailboard at the Leddy Park Beach.

Residential neighborhoods resume beyond the park, and in less than a mile spectacular views suddenly open up off to the left. A small sitting area has been developed, made especially for people to stop and enjoy the view. If you haven't taken advantage of the beaches yet, an extensive staircase system will take you down to another sandy beach—just remember that you'll eventually have to climb back up the stairs to get back to the trail.

Another sitting area has been developed in less than a half-mile. Soon after crossing North Avenue at grade, the bikeway ends at the Winooski River.

Imagine traversing a path built of tons of marble and rock fill, allowing you to bike, walk, or wheelchair several miles onto Lake Champlain. The Causeway Park Rail-Trail is among the most remarkable rail-trails in the country.

Activities:

Location: Chittenden County

Length: 3.2 miles

Surface: Packed gravel

Wheelchair access: Yes

Difficulty: Easy

Food: The town of Colchester is just a couple of miles away and has restaurants, fast-food establishments, and convenience stores.

Rest rooms: Airport Park

Seasons: Open year-round.

Access and parking: From Route 127, take Porters Point Road to Airport Road. Turn left onto Airport Road. About 0.25 mile beyond is a small parking lot. The trail begins on the other side of the street.

Rentals:
- Earl's Cycling & Fitness, 135 Main Street, Burlington, VT; (802) 862–4203.
- Vermont's Outdoor Sports Headquarters, 85 Main Street, Burlington, VT; (802) 658–3313.
- North Star Cyclery,100 Main Street, Burlington, VT; (802) 863–3832.

Transportation: Chittendon County Transit Authority, North Avenue Route. All CCTA vehicles have bicycle racks.

Contact: Town of Colchester Parks and Recreation Department, P.O. Box 55, Colchester, VT 05446; (802) 655–0811.

• •

The history of the Causeway Trail is one of persistence and determination. In the late 1800s, the Rutland Canada Railroad decided to build a railroad bed across Lake Champlain to allow rail traffic between Vermont and Canada. They built the bed using mar-

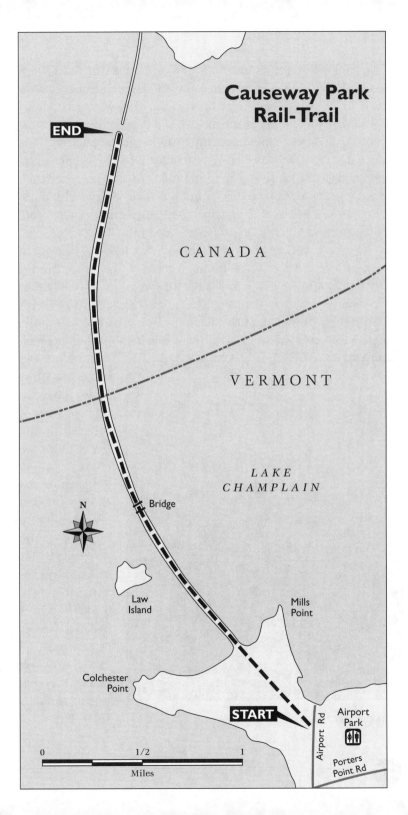

Causeway Park
Rail-Trail

END

CANADA

VERMONT

LAKE
CHAMPLAIN

N

Bridge

Law
Island

Mills
Point

Colchester
Point

START

Airport Rd

Airport
Park

Porters
Point Rd

0   1/2   1
Miles

ble slag and waste from mining pits. It took almost two years (from 1898 to the turn of the century) to complete the project. For close to sixty years, the trains continued to cross the causeway, carrying an assortment of products between the two countries. However, in 1967 the railway was closed and for nearly thirty years the causeway was neglected. In the early 1990s, a group of local residents banded together to make the causeway into a multiple use, nonmotorized trail. The path meets ADA standards for full access for people with physical limitations. There is some talk of building a drawbridge to connect the causeway to the Grand Island side of the trail.

It's a good idea here to carry a light-weight windbreaker, even in the warmth of summer. Once on the causeway, the winds can get pretty fierce. And while the trail is flat, the wind can force bikers to move more slowly than they would on a less exposed path.

From the parking lot, cross the street at the marked crosswalk. The path traverses a dense forest for the first half-mile before open-

Canada beckons across the way.

ing up to the causeway. Views of the lake are on both sides of the trail. To the left is Law Island.

Once on the causeway, you are literally 10 feet above the water. At 1.3 miles, a reconstructed railroad bridge passes over a cut in the causeway. At 2.0 miles, a bench made of marble is on the left side. This is a

A sailboat glides along Lake Champlain.

perfect place to stop and enjoy the view. Several murals painted on marble slabs by local artist Joe Mitros depict the views from the causeway, including the Green Mountains in the distance.

Many kinds of birds live in and around the causeway. It's a favorite stopover for ducks migrating from Canada, and duck hunting is permitted for a short period of time each fall. Use caution during the season. Great blue herons are also commonly seen in the area.

Take a moment at 2.5 miles to view the discarded railroad ties on the side of the causeway. The trail continues for another 0.7 mile. It is at its most spectacular at the end of the trail, at 3.2 miles. The Grand Isle portion of the causeway can be seen here just 100 yards away across the water. Undeveloped, it looks oddly forlorn. Various small fishing boats and sailboats make their way through the cut before venturing farther onto the lake.

29   Central Vermont Rail-Trail

You'll need a sense of adventure to get the most from this trail, which is not yet fully developed. The stunning Vermont scenery, however, may lure people to the trail despite its rough surface.

Activities:

Location: Franklin County

Length: 27 miles

Surface: Original ballast, ranging from loose gravel to fist-sized rocks

Wheelchair access: Limited

Difficulty: Difficult

Food: There are restaurants in St. Albans and along the trail in Sheldon Springs and Sheldon Junction, River Rapids, Enosburg Falls, East Berkshire, and Richford.

Rest rooms: Rest rooms are available at Lester's General Store in Rail City, Marge's Snack Shop in Sheldon Springs, Top Cat Motorsports in Sheldon Junction, at various establishments in Enosburg Falls, at Dick and Pam's Market in East Berkshire, and at various establishments in Richford.

Seasons: Open year-round.

Access and parking: From I-89, take exit 19 and follow the signs to Route 7 north. Turn right and travel 2 miles into St. Albans. Parking is available on the southeast corner of the intersection of Routes 7 and 105. The trail begins on the northern side of Route 105, just beyond the intersection. Look for the green and yellow rail-trail sign.

Rentals:
- Duke's Sport Shop, 17 Lake Street, St. Albans, VT; (802) 527-7127.
- Vermont Outdoor Sports, Inc., 748 Sheldon Road, St. Albans, VT; (802) 524-3892.

Contact: Northwest Rail-Trail Council, c/o Northwest Regional Planning Commission, 140 South Main Street, St. Albans, VT 05478; (802) 524-5958.

• • • • • • • • • • • • • • • • • • • •

K nown as "Rail City," St. Albans had seventeen railroad lines in its industrial heyday and was the headquarters of the Central Vermont Railroad for more than a century. However, the city's biggest

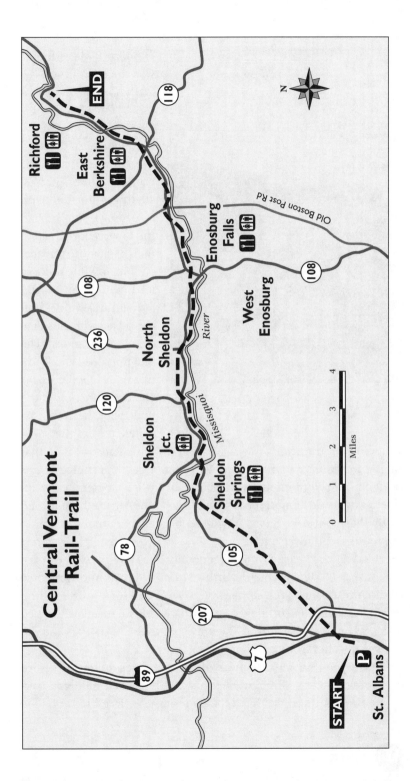

The Missisquoi River parallels the Central Vermont Rail-Trail's western half.

claim to fame is that it was the site of the Civil War's northernmost skirmish. On October 19, 1864, more than twenty Confederate soldiers led the "St. Albans Raid," robbing three banks, stealing horses, and spreading terror through the town before making their getaway to Canada.

The rail line to Richford hauled primarily agricultural freight and connected with the Canadian Pacific Railroad. The line remained active until a train derailed near Sheldon Junction in the mid-1980s, destroying a bridge over the Missisquoi River. Ironically, it was a Boston & Maine Railroad train that caused the damage to the Central Vermont bridge: the company was using the corridor temporarily because an earlier accident had damaged its own corridor. At the urging of snowmobilers in the state, led by the Vermont Area Snow Travelers, the state eventually acquired the route as a multiuse trail.

Heading northeast, farmland generally lines the route. The crossing under I–89 signals your departure from St. Albans into Vermont's rural countryside. Take some time to stop and look at the rolling farmland. There are cornfields and wildflower-filled meadows framed by a mountainous backdrop. The only sounds are bird songs and the hum of distant farm machinery.

Just before the 3.5-mile mark, the trail crosses Route 105 before beginning a steady climb into a forest. Within a half-mile you pass by an area on the right that appears to have suffered a fire and is now a wetland. The wetland supports a variety of wildlife, including Canada geese, wood ducks, great blue herons, muskrats, beavers, and a chorus of frogs. Other wildlife, like black bears, moose, deer, and marsh hawks, use this wetland for a part of their life cycle or during certain times of the year. Just after this area, a relatively young deciduous forest lines the trail on both sides. The entire region was logged extensively during the railroad era.

Near mile 5, the trail parallels a dirt road, which follows the trail corridor for the next couple of miles. This section remains a mix of woodlands and wildflowers with an occasional house. Soon the trail crosses Route 105 in Sheldon Springs, where you'll find a gas station and a convenience store. The views to the nearby mountains begin to open up at this point, as only a thin band of trees separates you from the surrounding scenery.

The trail meets up with Route 105 again at Sheldon Junction, nearly 9 miles into the journey. At this point, you see two-thirds of a trestle crossing the Missisquoi River. This is an eerie reminder of the debacle that caused the rail route's demise. To get around this seemingly permanent detour, take a left onto Route 105, cross the river, and take the first right. Weave your way through the Nutrite parking lot (over some remaining, although unused, railroad tracks) back to the Central Vermont corridor.

ST. ALBANS HISTORICAL MUSEUM

Housed in a renovated 1863 brick schoolhouse, the St. Albans Historical Museum features antique quilts, dolls, china, and glass and also displays an assortment of maps, photographs, and medical antiques. Railroad history buffs will be pleased to find railroad memorabilia. Of note is a furniture arrangement that duplicates the scene in Norman Rockwell's painting Family Doctor's Office. A signed print of the painting and the furniture was donated to the museum by the doctor whom Rockwell painted. Located at the intersection of Church and Bishops Streets, the museum is open on weekday afternoons throughout the summer and by appointment during the rest of the year. For more information, call (802) 527–7933.

From here all the way to Richford, the trail basically parallels Route 105. Within 1.5 miles the views suddenly reveal the rocky Missisquoi River below and to the right. In another half-mile the trail passes a restaurant, the last chance for a bite to eat for several miles.

Before mile 12, the trail crosses Route 105 and heads away from the river and into a lightly wooded area. Mountains and farms dominate the landscape, offering only a fleeting view of the river. Within 2 miles, the trail once again crosses Route 105, continuing to traverse farmland. Just before mile 13, the trail reaches Route 236. This is the trail's midway point and perhaps a turnaround point for all but the hardiest souls.

At this point, the trail is surrounded by cornfields. Mountain biking is truly a challenge and even hiking is difficult as the trail is rocky. By mile 16, the trail enters Enosburg Falls. The dairy industry has long been important in this area; Enosburg Falls was at one time referred to as the "Dairy Center of the World." Take note of the Victorian architecture of the town. If you are not already on Route 105, you should get on it for the next half-mile to avoid a bridge with no decking or handrails.

When you get to Main Street, you will find several shops, restaurants, and antiques stores. Turn right and then make a left onto Depot Street to get back to the trail.

The trail crosses Route 105 several more times in the next section. The views open to rolling farmland with an occasional view of the river. About 5 miles from Richford, the trail is surrounded by corn. In another 2 miles, the trail approaches a trestle over the Missisquoi River. Ties remain in place here, enabling you to cross the bridge.

Although the trail continues for a short interval after the trestle, it becomes less scenic. Within another mile, Route 105 also veers away from the trail. Power lines parallel the corridor before the trail ends in the town of Richford, whose early settlers were wilderness pioneers who smuggled products to Canada as their primary livelihood in the early nineteenth century.

At this point you are just a couple miles from the Canadian border. Future plans call for developing a trail across the international border and ultimately all the way to Montreal.

If you want to escape the hectic pace of most urban areas of the Northeast, plan a trip to the Delaware & Hudson Rail-Trail. Currently tucked along the rural western border of Vermont, the Delaware & Hudson Rail-Trail eventually will be a 34.3-mile trail straddling southwestern Vermont and part of New York State. Despite the fact that the two sections of the trail in Vermont are separated by 15 undeveloped miles in New York, the peaceful and unhurried setting of the "D&H" make the trip more than worthwhile.

Activities:

Location: Rutland County

Length: 9.2 miles

Surface: Original ballast, ranging from hard-packed cinder to gravel. The trail, although graded, may be too soft for the narrow tires found on most road bikes. *Note:* All motorized vehicles, including ATVs and dirt bikes, are prohibited.

Wheelchair access: None

Difficulty: Moderate

Food: Several restaurants are located at each end of the trail—in Poultney and in Castleton.

Rest rooms: None

Seasons: Open year-round.

Access and parking: From the junction of I–91 and I–89, take I–89 north 3 miles to exit 1 (Route 4). Turn left, continue 54 miles on Route 4, and exit at Castleton (exit 5). Turn left onto Route 4A. After 0.5 mile you will reach Castleton College. Turn left into the college entrance (Seminary Street). Pass several college buildings before turning right into the visitor parking area. Proceed to the end of the lot; a row of parking spaces to the right are designated D&H Trail parking spaces. The trailhead is adjacent to the row of parking spaces.

Rentals: Battenkill Sports Bicycle Shop, 1240 Depot Street, Manchester Center, VT; (802) 362–2734.

Contact: Gary Salmon, Forester/Trails Coordinator, Vermont Agency of Natural Resources, Department of Forests, Parks and Recreation, 317 Sanitorium Road, West Wing, Pittsford, VT 05763-9358; (802) 483–2733; fax (802) 483–9374; gary.salmon@anrmail.anr.state.vt.us.

* *

This area wasn't always as quiet as it is today. The history of this railroad line is deeply rooted in the once-bustling slate industry. The Delaware & Hudson Railroad constructed this corridor in the mid-1800s. Squares of high-quality red, green, and purple "roof that never wears out" were shipped to market throughout New York and the Northeast. The line quickly became known as the "Slate Picker," and in 1890 alone it carried 170,000 squares of slate from the area. Dairy farmers also made use of the line, as did passengers until the need for passenger service fell sharply during the Depression.

As trucks gained popularity, the "Slate Picker" suffered a slow but steady decline. The last train ran on the line in 1983. Vermont purchased its sections of the corridor with plans to operate a short-line railroad. This plan, however, never quite materialized, and with assistance from the Vermont Association of Snow Travelers, the state began converting its sections of the line into a trail in the late 1980s.

Remnants of the slate industry still line the trail.

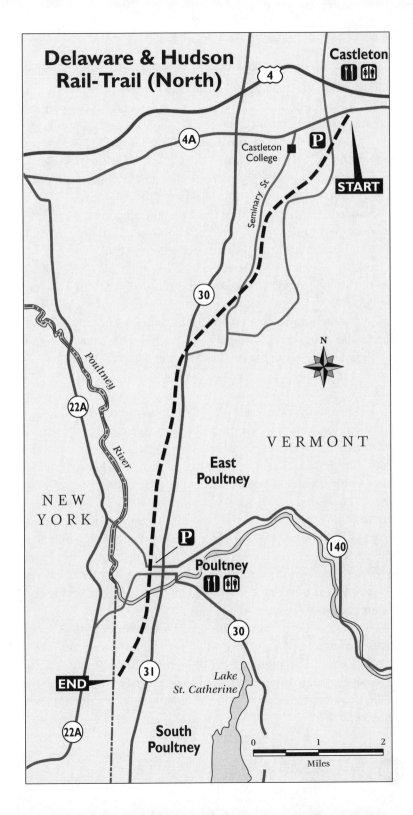

Upon completion of seventeen bridges, the northern and southern sections of the rail-trail opened in the early 1990s.

The rail-trail is managed by the Department of Forests, Parks and Recreation with assistance from the Vermont Association of Snow Travelers. A D&H Trails Advisory Council was formed in 1996 to help preserve the public right-of-way on the D&H for future transportation use by maintaining it for recreational uses for the present. The Council has been quite active in promoting the rail-trail.

Because it's uncertain when the 14.5-mile section in New York will open, this trail is covered in two sections—see "Delaware & Hudson Trail (South)" for the southern section of the trail.

From the Castleton College parking lot, the trail heads south, passing through mixed woods of white pine, willow, red oak, and sugar maple. At 0.3 mile, at the fork to the left, there is a remnant of an old switching station where trains once turned around. The trail surface, made up of hard-packed cinder, is quite smooth in this area. Farmland generally surrounds the trail, although if you pay attention you will see a few relics of the slate industry.

Just beyond the 1-mile mark, the path crosses the first of eighteen legal agricultural crossings. While these are used sporadically, use caution—especially if you hear farm machinery. The trail temporarily narrows to a single-track setting, but widens out again by the 2-mile mark. Here, you notice plenty of American beech trees as well as some Eastern hemlocks, which attract deer to the area.

In another half-mile, the trail passes a rock cut before entering an area of wetlands, to the left of the trail for nearly half a mile. Beyond the 3.5-mile mark is a large pond to the left, created by recent beaver activity. Take a moment to look for recently felled trees (or a beaver at work). A bridge just ahead offers a nice spot to rest and look for beavers.

The trail crosses busy Route 30 at grade soon after the 4-mile mark. During the summer, a small blue wildflower, known as chicory, lines the trail's edge. The highway parallels the trail's left side all the way into Poultney, although most of the time Route 30 is barely visible. Farm fields outlined by low mountains create bucolic views on the right.

After the 5.5-mile mark, the trail passes through a stand of aspen trees, which are often mistaken for white birches. Another wetland lines the trail's left side. Beavers and woodchucks may be spotted in this area, which is also dotted with a mix of colorful wildflowers.

In another mile, the trail enters the town of Poultney, where a small park surrounds the trail as you approach the depot. Poultney has a small-town atmosphere and several restaurants and shops.

As the trail continues, you soon cross one of the trail's longest bridges, nearly 100 feet. The approach to the bridge is quite rough, as large ballast was used to fill an area that suffered flood damage.

At 9.2 miles, the trail reaches the New York border. Here you will see a small, cryptic sign that says EXPLOSIVES. It is a warning that explosives are still used at a nearby active quarry, easily visible on the left side. The quarry is located in New York, and while the corridor appears open for some distance, it is technically not open for trail use at this time. The southern section of Vermont's Delaware & Hudson Trail resumes about 15 miles south of Poultney.

A fallen tree, an obvious indication of beaver activity.

A lightly wooded trail through cornfields and meadows of wild-flowers.

Activities:

Location: Rutland and Bennington Counties

Length: 10.6 miles

Surface: Original ballast, ranging from hard-packed cinder to gravel

Wheelchair access: Limited

Difficulty: Moderate

Food: Restaurants and markets are found in Poultney.

Rest rooms: None

Seasons: Open year-round.

Access and parking: From U.S. Route 4, take State Route 30 south through Poultney. About 11 miles south of Poultney, the road veers to the right onto Route 153, where a sign indicates that you are 3 miles from West Pawlet. As you approach the town, you will see obvious signs of the slate industry, including huge piles of slate. When the road comes to a T, turn right and the rail corridor will be immediately on the right alongside a depot. Parking is available in the small gravel lot next to the depot.

Rentals: Battenkill Sports Bicycle Shop, 1240 Depot Street, Manchester Center, VT; (802) 362–2734.

Contact: Gary Salmon, Forester/Trails Coordinator, Vermont Agency of Natural Resources, Department of Forests, Parks and Recreation, 317 Sanitorium Road, West Wing, Pittsford, VT 05763-9358; (802) 483–2733; fax (802) 483–9374; gary.salmon@anrmail.anr.state.vt.us.

• •

This scenic rail-trail is a pure delight. The trail traverses cornfields and meadows, with views of the nearby mountains.

You are now just inside the Vermont border and will want to head left on the trail, immediately crossing over this section's longest bridge. Within a half-mile, the Vermont scenery is particularly stunning. Here you will find vast fields of corn, which give

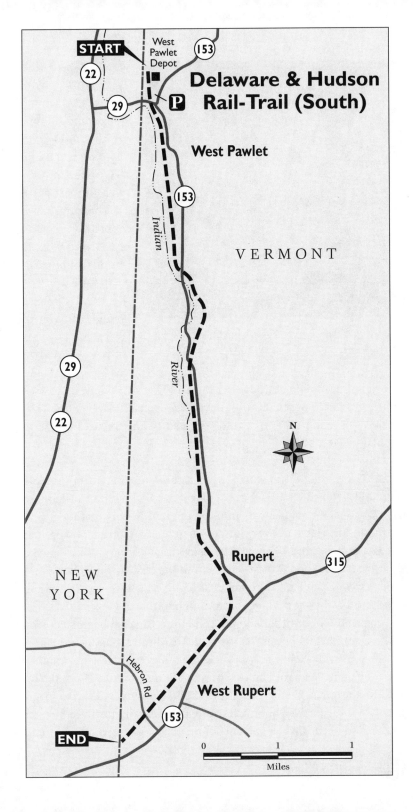

An occasional break in the trees reveals a view of a nearby farm.

way to rolling hillsides, only to be overtaken by much steeper mountains.

The trail generally parallels Route 153 (on the left) for most of its length, but the rural landscapes on the right keep your eyes happily occupied. At about 2.5 miles, the trail crosses Route 153 from West Pawlet. Although the trail is wooded in this area, you begin getting glimpses of the Indian River on the right. The trail crosses Route 153 again at the 4-mile mark. Use caution here as the trail crosses the road in a fairly blind spot and motorists have no warning of a trail crossing.

On the other side of Route 153 the trail resumes its tree-lined route. The path continues to parallel mountains on the right, while cornfields alternate with fallow fields on the left. Within a little more than 2 miles, the path heads into the town of Rupert, with wonderful mountain vistas in every direction. The town offers no services but is a picturesque tiny hamlet. Leaving town, the trail crosses a short bridge. Beyond Rupert, views from the trail become even more spectacular. Corn stalks are about the only vegetation surrounding the corridor, thus providing panoramic mountain views. Route 153 runs close by the trail for about a mile until the trail begins veering to the right. At this point, the town of West Rupert comes into view.

After crossing Hebron Cross Road, the trail continues about another half-mile to the New York border, passing through farmlands for the remaining distance. The corridor ahead gets progressively more overgrown and the bridges are impassable. It is uncertain whether or not this section of the former rail corridor will be converted into a trail.

32 Montpelier and Wells River Rail-Trail

The Montpelier and Wells River Rail-Trail offers panoramic views of the Vermont mountains and is quite spectacular. But it may take some effort as the trail is at its best once you have traveled uphill for more than 5 miles.

Activities:

Location: Caledonia County

Length: 14.5 miles

Surface: Original ballast, ranging from sand to a mix of course gravel and dirt

Wheelchair access: None

Difficulty: Difficult

Food: Best bet is to find a restaurant or grocery in Montpelier or Barre before going to the trail.

Rest rooms: Ricker, Big Deer, and Stillwater campgrounds

Seasons: Open year-round.

Access and parking: From I–91, take a left at exit 17 onto U.S. Route 302 west toward Groton. About 5 miles past Groton, take a right onto Route 232 north (also known as Groton Forest Highway). Travel 1.6 miles north to a parking lot near Ricker Pond on the right side of the road. Park here and plan to head north after taking in some views of Ricker Pond. The trail technically continues back to Route 302 (on the opposite side of 232), but offers little of interest.

Rentals:
- Onion River Sports, 20 Langdon Street, Montpelier, VT; (802) 229–9409.
- Onion River Sports, 395 North Main Street, Barre, VT; (802) 476–9750.

Contact: David Willard, Trails Coordinator, Vermont Agency of Natural Resources, Department of Forests, Parks and Recreation, 184 Portland Street, St. Johnsbury, VT 05819-2099; (802) 751–0110; fax (802) 748–6687.

. . . .

The bad news is that in order to really appreciate this trail, you must go uphill for most of its 14.5 miles. The good news is that the views at the top are well worth the trouble you've taken; besides, getting back will seem comparatively effortless.

The area that now makes up Vermont's Groton State Forest has a long history, beginning with the Abenaki Indians who are believed to have camped and hunted there. Later, explorers moved through the region, with the first white settlers arriving after the American Revolution. The land was deemed too rugged for farming but ideal for logging. It didn't take long for several mills to begin operating in the town of Groton.

By 1873, the Montpelier and Wells River Railroad had opened to serve the mills and to provide a connection between the Central Vermont and the Boston & Maine Railroads. The Montpelier and Wells also brought passengers to the area, many seeking places to camp and swim along the scenic shores of Lake Groton. Virtually every virgin tree in the area was logged by the 1920s, although the rail line remained in service until 1956. The Groton State Forest is now Vermont's second-largest contiguous landholding, with some 25,000 acres. With the growth of a crop of new trees, the land is used extensively for recreational purposes.

The parking lot was originally home to one of the nation's oldest continuously running sawmills, operating from 1857 to 1963. The trail here is a mix of sand and gravel, with occasional sharp rocks protruding through the surface.

Within 0.3 mile, the trail passes a gate, signaling the entrance to Ricker Campground, which has thirty tent sites and several lean-tos, rest rooms, and drinking water. Take a right at the fork in the trail and leave the campground through a second gate.

Just after 1 mile, the trail passes Depot Brook Trail, where an informational kiosk outlines many of the snowmobiling trails. At the 2-mile mark the trail crosses over a second dirt road, which leads to a new lakefront development. The trail is lined on both sides with a forest of young maple, beech, and oak, with occasional aspen and white pine trees.

Lake Groton will come into view on the right within a half-mile, while a rocky embankment lines the left side. The trail continues to ascend, but the surface gets rougher in this section. After 3 miles, a sign on the left indicates a scenic view. This is a perfect time to stop to enjoy the view of the lake.

In another half-mile, the trail reaches a paved road that leads

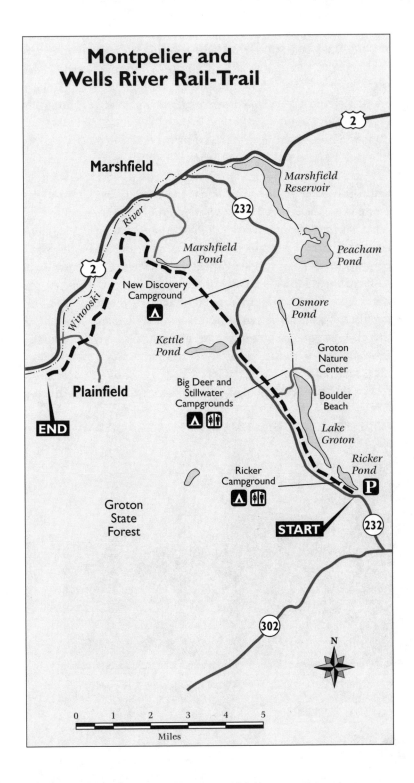

to the Big Deer and Stillwater Campgrounds, a nature center, picnic tables, and Boulder Beach. If you take the road to the right, within 2 miles (mostly downhill) you reach Boulder Beach, where there are picnic tables in a wonderfully scenic setting along the shores of Lake Groton.

Once back on the trail, you pass the former site of Peabody's Mill on the right. About 5 miles into the journey, the trail crosses a small bridge, while continuing to climb uphill. Soon you cross another paved road, which is the main forest road (Route 232). The views open up dramatically to the towering mountains on the right.

Douglas fir trees line the trail's left side before a mix of deciduous and evergreen trees again overtake the corridor. By mile 6, the forest canopy again opens up, offering spectacular views of the sheer granite cliffs of Owl's Head Mountain on the right. You can reach the top of Owl's Head thanks to members of the Civilian Conservation Corps, who built the road to the right and the short trail leading to the top. From this lofty vantage point, you literally get a bird's-eye view of the lakes and forest, with the trail running straight through the middle.

The rail-trail soon crosses a lightly traveled road at grade. Goldenrod, milkweed, and wild daisies now accent the trail's perimeter,

The sheer granite cliffs of Owl's Head Mountain command your attention in the trail's midsection.

while patches of wetland dot the surrounding landscape. Occasional boulders poke through the trail's rutted surface in the vicinity of mile 7. Beyond this point, trees again begin to shroud the trail, which temporarily narrows. The trail soon offers views of Marshfield Pond. By the 8-mile mark, the surface improves significantly and the mountain views are spectacular. Be sure to look to your right—and occasionally over your shoulder—to catch the panoramic views. The surface is moderately rough in this section.

The wide surface of the Montpelier and Wells River Rail-Trail provides ample room for everyone to enjoy the trail.

Just less than 9 miles from the beginning of the trail, you arrive at another fork. The branch to the right (where you will see a 35 miles-per-hour sign posted) is a road, while the railroad corridor continues on the left. The trail gets a bit sandy in this section, and generally seems more lightly used than earlier sections of the trail. Trees form a canopy overhead, with dense forest off to the left and an occasional clearing on the right.

At about 9.5 miles, the trail reaches another fork, again continuing to the left. You will find a gate here; all recreational users are welcome to proceed along the trail. (The gate was put up to prevent people from driving cars on the trail and camping along the corridor.)

The trail continues for more than 3 miles, curving west and then southwest for its remaining distance. The trail passes several clearings and logging roads as it wends its way toward the Winooski River. The trail ends before reaching the river, but you may be able to hear it off to your right.

MORE RAIL-TRAILS

This trail is for the hardy hiker willing to climb over a fallen tree or two. The payoff is the Lye Brook Falls at the end of the trail.

Activities:

Location: Bennington County

Length: 5 miles

Surface: Varies, but primarily packed dirt. Deadfalls are apt to block the trail in places.

Wheelchair access: None

Difficulty: Moderate

Food: There are numerous restaurants and food stores in nearby Manchester.

Rest rooms: None

Seasons: Summer

Access and parking: To get to the trail, take a right at the light at the intersection of Routes 11 and 30. Turn right onto Richville Road, then east onto Manchester Road. Pass under the underpass of Route 7, then turn right on Glenn Road. Go straight onto Lye Brook Road and follow it to the trailhead parking lot.

Rentals: None

Contact: Greg Wright, Green Mountain National Forest, 231 North Main Street, Rutland, VT 05701-2412; (802) 747–6700.

Various lumber ventures took place in the Green Mountains, with local railroad service providing the means of bringing fallen trees to the mills. Smack dab in the middle of the Green Mountain Range and just minutes away from the resort community of Manchester, the Lye Brook Falls Rail-Trail offers a pleasant hike through forest and leads to a waterfall. A 5-mile hike, the trail experiences a 600-foot elevation gain. The trail follows an old logging railroad grade and wood roads. At several points in the trail, toppled trees from past storms make the trail impassable unless you're willing to scramble over or around them. For hardy hikers, it's a worthwhile trip to Lye Brook Waterfall at the end of the trail.

The Lye Brook Falls trail is located in the beautiful Green Mountains region of Vermont.

West River Rail-Trail

Several paths are available at the West River Rail-Trail, including a 3-mile-long path that follows the old railroad bed through the woods.

Activities:

Location: Windham County

Length: 3 miles

Surface: Paved through the park, then gravel for the remainder of the trail

Wheelchair access: Yes. For the heartier wheelchair-bound individual, the trails can be a lot of fun.

Difficulty: Moderate

Food: There are no restaurants in Jamaica State Park. The best bet is to stop in Brattleboro for provisions before heading out on the rail-trail.

Rest rooms: In the campgrounds

Seasons: Campgrounds are only open in the summer months; however, the trails are open year-round.

Access and parking: From I–91, take exit 2 to Route 9. Turn left. Continue on Route 9 for 18 miles until you reach the town of Wilmington. Look for Route 100 in the center of downtown. Take a right onto Route 100 and proceed for 20 miles until you reach Route 30. The entrance to Jamaica State Park is located on the right, 0.5 mile past the center of town, on Depot Street.

Rentals:

- Equipe Sport, 22 Mount Snow Access Road, West Dover, VT; (802) 464–2222.
- Mountain Riders, junction of Routes 30 and 100, South Londonderry, VT; (802) 297–1745.

Contact: Rick White, Trail Coordinator, Vermont Agency of Natural Resources, Department of Forests, Parks and Recreation, 100 Mineral Street Suite 304, Springfield, VT 05156; (802) 885–8824.

• •

The West River Railroad began running from South Londonderry to Brattleboro in 1881. Numerous floods and storms created such havoc that the railroad was nicknamed "the railroad of 36 miles of trouble."

Located in Jamaica State Park, the West River Rail-Trail is a 3-mile trail good for walking, jogging, or biking. The park comprises 772 acres of mixed hardwoods and hemlock, white pine, red spruce, elm, and ash. Wildlife includes deer, beavers, and grouse. The trail follows the West River along the bed of the West River Railroad. Look for the Dumplings, a group of large boulders about a half-mile up the trail. In another 2 miles, the trail reaches Cobb Brook. After crossing the brook, the trail's final destination is the Ball Mountain Dam, standing 265 feet high and 915 feet long.

The nearby Hamilton Falls Trail is also worthy of note. Follow the West River Rail-Trail for 2.5 miles. Before reaching Cobb Brook, the trail intersects the old switch road. Bear right and continue up the switch road for about a mile. A steep footpath on the left will take you to the bottom of the falls. To go to the top of the falls, continue on the switch road to the end, turn left past the Hamilton Falls Lumber Mill, then turn left onto a steep path. From here you can look down at the 125-foot cascade. Day use at Jamaica State Park is $2.00 per adult and $1.50 per child.

Future Vermont Rail-Trails

Vermont, like the rest of New England, has been rallying behind the rails-to-trails movement and working on expanding the number of trails in the state. In Springfield, a 3-mile bicycle trail is in the final planning stages. The trail will follow the corridor of the abandoned Springfield Terminal Railway between Springfield and the Cheshire Bridge over the Connecticut River.

An additional 37.9 miles of trail is proposed between Montpelier and Wells River (Montpelier and Wells River Rail-Trail).

In the town of Rochester, a citizen's group in the town is interested in establishing the Peavine Trail, which would use the old railroad bed passing through the town.

Also of interest is the Lake Champlain Bikeways Initiative to create a network of interconnected and international bicycle routes on existing roads around Lake Champlain in New York, Vermont, and the Upper Richelieu Valley in Quebec. Over 350 miles of route around the entire lake in Vermont and New York, and along the Richelieu River to Chambly, Quebec, have been identified and mapped. Although the Burlington Waterfront Bikeway is the only part of the trail associated with a railroad, the Rails-to-Trails Conservancy is one of the major advocates for this initiative.

TrailLink.com

Linking you to the best trails in the nation.

Rails-to-Trails Conservancy is proud
to present **TrailLink.com,** your one
stop trail travel service.

Your FREE companion service to the official Rails-to-Trails Conservancy guidebook series

➤ Over 1,000 trails for walking, running, biking, in-line
skating, horseback riding, and cross-country skiing

➤ More than 11,000 miles of trails all over the U.S.

➤ Regularly updated information on trails and trail activities

➤ Detailed information on trail access, parking, surfaces,
and more

➤ Links to local trail organization Web sites and useful trail
resources

*The Best Coverage Of Multi-use Pathways
On The Internet*

RAILS-TO-TRAILS CONSERVANCY • *Connecting People and Communities*

FREE T!*

*with a $50 contribution or more

100% cotton T-shirt with Rails-to-Trails Conservancy logo printed on the front; and a circle of trail users printed in royal blue on back.

JOIN RAILS-TO-TRAILS CONSERVANCY NOW, get a FREE T-SHIRT and connect yourself with the largest national trail-building organization. As a member of Rails-to-Trails Conservancy, you will receive the following benefits:

- *Rails to Trails*, a colorful magazine dedicated to celebrating trails and greenways, published four times a year
- A free copy of *Sampler of America's Rail-Trails*
- Discounts on publications, merchandise and conferences
- A free t-shirt with your contribution of $50 or more
- Additional membership benefits for Trailblazer Society members, including invitation to the annual rail-trail excursions

Most importantly, you will have the satisfaction that comes from helping to build a nationwide network of beautiful trails for all of us to enjoy for years and generations to come.

PLEASE JOIN TODAY by calling toll-free: 1-800-888-7747, ext. 11(credit card orders only), or mail your membership contribution with the form on the following page, or see our web site, **www.railtrails.org**.

RAILS-TO-TRAILS CONSERVANCY • *Connecting People and Communities*

Yes! I want to join Rails-to-Trails Conservancy!

Send me my member packet, including my *Sampler of America's Rail-Trails,* one year (four issues) of *Rails to Trails,* the colorful magazine that celebrates trails and greenways and my FREE T-SHIRT with my contribution of $50 or more. I will also receive discounts on publications, merchandise and conferences. Here is my membership gift of:

❏ $18 – Individual
❏ $25 – Supporting
❏ $50 – Patron *(Free t-shirt at this giving level or higher!)*

T-shirt size XL only

❏ $100 – Benefactor
❏ $500 – Advocate
❏ $1,000 – Trailblazer Society
❏ Other $_____

❏ Monthly Giving, *please see box below*

PAYMENT METHOD: ❏ VISA   ❏ MasterCard   ❏ American Express
Card # _____ Exp. Date_____
Signature _____
Member Name_____
Street _____
City _____ State _____ Zip _____
Telephone _____ email_____

Rails-to-Trails Conservancy is a non-profit charitable 501(c)(3) organization. Contributions are tax-deductible.

I want to support Rails-to-Trails Conservancy in the smartest, easiest and best way possible by donating monthly. Enclosed is my first monthly gift of:
  ❏ $5   ❏ $10   ❏ $15   ❏ Other $_____ *($5 minimum monthly contribution, please)*

Charge my future monthly gifts to my :
❏ Checking Account — Please transfer the amount indicated from my bank account each month
❏ Credit Card — Please charge the amount indicated to my credit card each month: ❏ VISA   ❏ MasterCard   ❏ American Express

Card Number: _____ Exp. Date: _____
Signature: _____ Date: _____

PAPERLESS PLEDGE AUTHORIZATION: I authorize Rails-to-Trails Conservancy to transfer my monthly contribution from my bank account or to charge my credit card (whichever I have indicated). I understand I may cancel or change my monthly pledge at any time by notifying Rails-to-Trails Conservancy. A record of each payment will appear on my monthly bank or credit card statement and will serve as my receipt.

Signature: _____ Date Signed: _____

EFT

Rails-to-Trails Conservancy
1100 17th St. NW • Washington, DC 20036
1-800-888-7747, ext. 11 (credit card orders only) • www.railtrails.org

To contact our membership department, please call (202) 974-5105 or email rtchelen@transact.org

RAILS TO TRAILS CONSERVANCY

GUIDE